FATAL
FALLACIES

How Ideologues Repeal the Laws of Logic

CW Griffin

ISBN: 978-1-4907-4901-3 (sc)
ISBN: 978-1-4907-4900-6 (hc)
ISBN: 978-1-4907-4899-3 (e)

Library of Congress Control Number: 2014918761

Trafford rev. 11/15/2014

 www.trafford.com

North America & international
toll-free: 1 888 232 4444 (USA & Canada)
fax: 812 355 4082

CONTENTS

PREFACE

In the unprecedented assault on science and logical thought afflicting the United States throughout the 21st-century's early years, the role of lies has been recognized, if not adequately exposed, by the general media. Largely ignored by the media, however, is the role of logical fallacies in perpetrating ideological nonsense. Vividly demonstrated by the stupefyingly idiotic Republican 2012 presidential primary, the assault on reason descended to previously unplumbed depths. Facts are suppressed, lies are endlessly repeated, and more importantly, logic is seldom, if ever, allowed to rear its presumably ugly head. Every fallacy in the logic textbooks, augmented by a few politically originated follies, is exploited to the fullest extent. As these logical fallacies have been almost totally ignored by the general media, my purpose in this book is to enumerate, explain, and illustrate these fallacies with numerous examples drawn from contemporary -- chiefly, political -- life.

Attempts at rational discussion are sometimes denounced, but more frequently ignored. Ideological myths are ferociously defended via one or more of the following fallacies:

- reversing the burden of proof
- the slippery slope
- nopanaceism
- straw men
- red herrings
- the vicious-circle
- single-entry bookkeeping
- language perversion

From the prevailing use of these fallacies we get the conservatives' mindless ideologies – notably, supply-side economics, free-lunch patriotism, pretended concern for education while suppressing instruction in biological science, the myth of liberally biased media, and other nonsense discussed in detail and exposed for its biased irrationality in this book's text.

The liberal-biased myth was spectacularly highlighted in several 2012 presidential primary debates involving CNN reporter John King acting as moderator. In the first instance, Newt Gingrich excoriated King for opening the debate with a perfectly legitimate, and timely, question. It requested Gingrich's response to his divorced second wife's charge that Gingrich had asked her to agree to an "open" marriage while he carried on an affair with his current wife, Callista. When the talented demagogue accused King of doing Obama's work by asking this question, the audience exploded in a riotous outburst exulting in Gingrich's denunciation of the mainstream media. King meekly accepted their emotion-laden verdict.

A second instance, also involving King, was far less dramatic, but, in my opinion, more significant. Again acting as moderator, King asked each of the four contenders to reveal his worst campaign error, the one he most wished he had avoided. Instead of responding to the question, Mitt Romney ignored it and repeated his standard political attack on President Obama. When King correctly intervened, charging Romney with evading the question, Romney indignantly defended his evasion. "You get to ask the questions, I get to answer them any way I want," was the gist of Romney's reply. "Fair enough," said King, thereby endorsing the candidates' prevalent practice of ducking debate questions with recited propaganda. If, as King acknowledged, candidates can ignore difficult or embarrassing questions asked at debates, what is the purpose of having a moderator asking these questions? It is difficult to imagine anything less interesting or less beneficial to the political process than allowing a candidate to simply repeat rehearsed political banalities without tackling tough issues. Yet, to my knowledge, no mainstream media representative asked this vitally important question: If candidates are free to ignore moderators' questions, why have moderators asking these questions?

Why not just drop the pretense that candidate forums are debates, eliminate the moderator, and simply allow candidates to recite propaganda?

King's cowardly response to Romney's bullying exposed as nonsense the perpetually parroted charge of liberal media bias. This conservative myth has been pounded into blockheads' brains through the constant repetition so effectively used by Hitler's propaganda minister Joseph Goebbels. What King's response exemplified was the mainstream media's fear of conservative attack and its general refusal to attack conservative propaganda and demand evidence for its reckless charges.

The profits from being outrageous raise the question whether Limbaugh, Hannity, and their fellow demagogues even believe their extreme views. Hannity provides a curious illustration. He never conceded the conclusion forced upon even the reluctant Bush administration, whose $1-billion search failed to turn up Saddam Hussein's alleged WMDs. According to Hannity, these missing WMDs were probably in Syria. But if Hannity seriously believed this speculation, then he would certainly have called for a challenge to Syria to give up these weapons. Instead he simply dropped the subject. Must we then conclude that Hannity saw nothing threatening in Syria's possession of WMDs? Or is it more likely that he saw no problem in Syria's possession of WMDs because he really didn't believe in it. He was merely stoking his paranoid listeners' suspicious fears. That, I think, is the most probable explanation for Hannity's Syrian weapon-possession thesis.

Limbaugh's faked beliefs include one particularly sleazy pretense, wherein he feigns tolerance for President Obama's presumed Muslim faith. In this cleverly fabricated scenario, he castigates Obama's secret commitment to Islam, not for the religious faith itself, but for Obama's alleged dishonesty in not avowing it. His gratuitous assumption that Obama is really a Muslim, despite his claim to be a Christian, involves the vicious-circle fallacy, which assumes the truth of a disputed fact without a scintilla of evidence. To the vicious-circle fallacy, Limbaugh adds the hypocrisy of pretended tolerance, knowing that he can count on his gullible audience to believe that Obama is, in fact, a Muslim.

Rightwing propagandists depend upon their audience's combined ignorance and hypocrisy to perpetrate their lucrative racket. Bible Belt conservatives' constant calls for limited government display an incredible degree of ignorance and hypocrisy. The nation's poorest state, Mississippi, is one of the most dependable sources of demands to limit government spending and "get government off people's backs," (except, of course, where women's reproductive rights are concerned). But Mississippi gets far more than a proportional share of federal dollars, far more than the average 25 percent excess -- $100 billion contributed by the higher income blue (i.e., Democratic) states to the poorer red (i.e., Republican) states. Polls have demonstrated the overwhelming support for Social Security and Medicare by the Tea Party members, the loudest protesters against federal spending. If by some political miracle, a Republican administration actually attempted to cut this federal spending, the protesting screams from their Bible Belt beneficiaries would reduce their current screams against abstract spending to comparative silence.

Self delusion is nonetheless minor compared with the general delusions afflicting the extremists. Evidence-based therapy, an indispensable part of any effort to reduce the nation's staggering $2-trillion annual medical bill, is viciously attacked by Tea Partiers and other conservative Republicans as "death panels." Despite currently pervasive health-care rationing, honest recognition of this inescapable fact is greeted with outraged protests.

It is sometimes mistakenly inferred that the Tea Partiers have introduced new ideas into American politics. This is a delusion. Writing in the nineteenth century, historian Frederick Jackson Turner showed how the frontier fostered the anti-social, tax-hating sermons preached by Tea Party leaders. In his perceptive essay, "The Paranoid Style in American Politics," historian Richard Hofstadter traced anti-intellectualism back to its colonial origins in the slave states. If there is any novelty in contemporary ideological extremism, it entails the evangelical Christians' hypocrisy, preaching "family values" while giving their support to the sleazy serial adulterer, Newt Gingrich, who has the brazen gall to hold himself up as exemplar of virtue. Accompanying the intellectual vacuum characterizing these demented ideologues there is an equally immense moral vacuum as well.

In the 2012 Republican presidential primary, we saw a uniquely perverse display of opportunism by the victor, Mitt Romney. The record is there for all to see, in graphic living color and sound: Romney's promiscuous flipflopping on abortion, health care, global warming, gun control, immigration, TARP stimulus, stem-cell research, and gay rights. For the nation's largest television news outlet, Fox News, Romney's flipflopping was predictably ignored. In England, however, Fox News's owner, Robert Murdoch's corruption, his bribery of the police and cell-phone hacking, have exacted huge costs from his propaganda empire. Meanwhile in the United States, Murdoch continues unabated, pedaling extremist propaganda, mangling facts, and violating the laws of logic with impunity. Fox News's gullible American audience has no counterpart among the world's dominant democracies.

CHAPTER 1

Ideology Triumphant

"All philosophers who find
Some favorite system to their mind.
In every point to make it fit,
Will force all nature to submit."

Thomas Love Peacock

Perhaps the most astonishing aspect of the Information Age, when arcane facts can be accessed merely by pushing a computer button, is the colossal ignorance pervading contemporary politics. In the early years of the 21st century America's polarized politics reminds us that historical progress does not proceed in a smooth, continuous trajectory. It stumbles through the centuries on an erratic course, with prominent peaks and valleys. As an extreme example, Europe's Dark Ages thrust European civilization back into Bronze-Age ignorance after the tremendous advances of the

1

Graeco-Roman era. It took about 12 centuries to elevate British law back to the fourth-century stage of Roman law that had governed the colony's more civilized parts. (As a noteworthy example of its reactionary culture, Dark-Age Britain abandoned Roman law's innocent-until-proven-guilty principle, introduced by the Stoic emperor Antonius Pius in the second century C.E.)

On what we can hope is a smaller scale, we are experiencing a political Dark Age in the stupefying polarization of contemporary American politics. Displaying ignorance far beyond the call of ideological duty, economically illiterate Tea Party fanatics were willing to risk a federal debt default in October, 2013. Some even argued that a government default might benefit our economy. Economists overwhelmingly reject this preposterous notion, arguing that a U.S. government default, undermining the world's dominant currency, would be an unalleviated catastrophe.

Associated with this willful, aggressive ignorance is the normalization of extreme rhetoric. Ferocious opposition to health-alcare reform has driven conservatives into mindless hyperbole that would merit hostile ridicule in a rational society. According to Senator Rand Paul, a leading candidate for the 2016 Republican presidential nomination, belief in "the right to health care" is "basically saying you believe in slavery." Paul's rhetoric drew Tea Party cheers. And in the House Committee on Science, Space and Technology, a subcommittee chairman claims that Evolution and Big-Bang cosmological theory are "straight from the pit of hell." That, too, drew no audible protest from his Republican colleagues.

Equally outlandish rhetorically, and paranoid besides, was venture capitalist Ron Perkin's assertion that American progressives' condemnation of bankers paralleled Nazi Germany's extermination of 6 million Jews. In 2010, Blackstone chief Stephen Schwartzman denounced President Obama's proposal to close a tax loophole that enables billionaire hedge-fund managers to pay a top tax rate roughly half their secretaries' top rate. This proposed loophole-closing "was like when Hitler invaded Poland in 1939," according to Schwartzman.

At its roots, political polarization marks the retrogressive triumph of ideological over scientific reasoning. Scientific reasoning has never been popular in politics. But as evidenced by their unanimous rejection of climatological science, even of biological science by some, the 2012 Republican presidential contenders fell to new depths of unscientific politics.

This chapter's epigraph by Thomas Love Peacock serves as an accurate definition of ideological reasoning. Ideology merely assumes the truth of some overpowering idea, adducing all the facts in its favor, but ignoring contradictory facts. Scientific reasoning accounts for all relevant facts. If a tested hypothesis is logically incompatible with any significant fact, it is rejected. On the contrary, ideological beliefs ignore all relevant facts that contradict their politically biased hypotheses. A notorious example is the durable, 30-year-old Arthur-Laffer myth that tax cuts always promote increased economic growth. Nobel prize-winning economist Paul Samuelson demolished that myth soon after it was publicized.

Ideological reasoning is obviously at its worst in the Third World. In South Africa, a recent president, Thebo Mbeki, clung for years to a stubborn denial that the HIV virus causes AIDs. Instead, President Mbeki banned scientifically proven antiretroviral drugs and subsidized worthless tribal "cures" based on primitive superstition. The causal link between HIV and AIDs was solidly established more than 30 years ago. But Mbeki still rejected it, as recently as 2008. During his tenure nearly one-fifth of South African adults were AIDs-infected, dying at a rate exceeding 900 daily. According to Harvard researchers, Mbeki's folly caused 365,000 unnecessary AIDs-caused deaths through his rejection of proven medical science.

Along with their superstitious rejection of science, South Afrikaners also found a scapegoat. Western drug companies and governments allegedly marketed toxic antiretroviral drugs, deliberately killing Africans. In 2000 Mbeki hinted at CIA involvement in propagating the allegedly false belief linking HIV with AIDs. Ignorance was compounded by paranoia.

Americans are spared this particular anti-scientific belief. But South Africa's anti-scientific outlook was less a retrogression than a persistence of traditional superstition, whereas anti-scientific attitudes in the U.S. represent retrogression.

Anti-scientific superstition has always had a congenial home in the former Confederacy. Battles rage over the teaching of Evolution throughout the Bible Belt and even in midwestern Kansas, where the state's highest ranking education administrator proudly proclaims his belief in a 6,000-year-old earth.

Anti-scientific attitudes are evident in the nation-wide battle over vaccines. A phony report written by a "researcher" with huge conflicts of interest is jeopardizing the eradication of several potentially serious childhood diseases. Those who profit from anti-scientific denial often fight on long after their pet theses have been forensically annihilated. As established anti-scientific deniers, they often have a profit motive to persist in denial.

Ideological Fuhrer

Like South Africa's HIV-causes-AIDs deniers, Rush Limbaugh is our most notorious global-warming denier. His underwhelming qualifications for challenging human-caused global warming include his record as a college dropout, a former disk jockey, and for a quarter century, an extravagantly paid (reputedly $60 million a year) professional demagogue duping millions of simple-minded, self-styled dittoheads with a litany of lies, misinformation, and logical fallacies. Limbaugh resembles South African HIV-causes-AIDs deniers in charging scientists with a gigantic conspiracy designed to destroy the U.S. economy. It's a precise parallel with South African AIDs deniers who charge Western scientists with the previously noted conspiratorial plot to kill Africans. Limbaugh never produces a single corroborating fact supporting his conspiracy hypothesis. He simply knows, with self-evident certainty, that human-caused global warming is a gigantic hoax.

Limbaugh's anti-scientific opinions range far beyond global-warming denial. He agrees with the fanatical opponent of

Evolution, Ben Stein, that the teaching of evolutionary biology led to the Holocaust. Limbaugh seldom, if ever, broadcasts this opinion. He has, however, published it in his newsletter. For some reason, either ignorance of his views, or possibly fear of offending Limbaugh's listeners, the nation's press has never probed the deaths of Limbaugh's ignorance. (In Chapter 7, I go into greater detail about Limbaugh's anti-scientific philosophy.)

The ultimate ideologue

The unparalleled exemplar of successful demagogic ideology is Adolph Hitler. As he informs us in his tedious tome, *Mein Kampf*, Hitler never had to open his mind to to reconsider anything. In his youth, he tells us:

> "... there took shape within me a world picture and a philosophy which became the granite foundation of all my acts. In addition to what I then created, I have had to learn little, and I have had to alter nothing."

Here's how historian Ian Kershaw poses the Hitler problem:

> "... not just how this initially most unlikely pretender to high state office could gain power; but how he was able to extend that power until it became absolute, until field marshals were prepared to obey without question the orders of a former corporal, until highly skilled 'professionals' and clever minds in all walks of life were ready to pay uncritical obeisance to an autodidact whose only indisputable talent was one for stirring up the masses."

Kershaw expands on this theme, describing Hitler's intellectual sloth:

> ". . . *Systematic preparation and hard work were as foreign to the young Hitler as they would be to the later dictator. Instead, his time was largely spent in dilettante faction . . . devising grandiose schemes shared only with the willing Kubizek —— fantasy plans that usually arose from sudden whims and bright ideas and were dropped almost as soon as they had begun.*"

What Hitler had, of course, was a prodigious talent for inflaming the masses. Because he himself shared their grievances, he unerringly identified their fears, paranoia, and resentments, cleverly stoking these psychic embers into raging flames. His was a remarkable talent for ridicule, sarcasm, and other rhetorical devices skillfully designed to evoke violent emotional responses from his cynically exploited victims. Far from disguising his contempt for the masses, Hitler freely expressed it:

> "*The receptivity of the masses is unlimited, their intelligence is small, but their power of forgetting is enormous.*"

This same cynical exploitation of his mass audience is manifest in Rush Limbaugh's appeal. His overwhelmingly male audience, predominantly bitter old men, harbors grievances against the elite, Ivy-school-educated elites. As the omniscient El Rushmo, dean of the fictitious Advanced School for Conservative Studies, Limbaugh purges doubt from his attacks on opponents. In Limbaugh's alternate universe, there is no possibility that global-warming is true, and that the scientists propounding the theory are not united in a vast conspiracy of lies. He projects absolute certainty on this and every other major political issue.

As I shall demonstrate in greater detail in Chapter 7, Limbaugh seldom allows contradictory facts to disrupt his theses. But even more characteristic of his modus operandi is his prolific use of a wide variety of logical fallacies. Back in the summer of 2008, when gas prices skyrocketed above $4 per gallon, Limbaugh blamed Democrats for the $4 gas. "Have you noticed," Limbaugh asks a befuddled caller, "that gas prices went up when Democrats took control of the House?"

This clumsy innuendo simultaneously embodies a lie and a violation of an elementary principle of formal logic. Skyrocketing gas prices are correlated with the Bush Administration's tenure. After dipping to an inflation-corrected $1.30 in 2002, gas prices climbed on an oscillating trajectory to $4-plus in June, 2008, tripling in six years. In Bush's eight years, gas prices more than doubled, a rate nearly three times the rise during the Clinton years. Limbaugh has no excuse for not recognizing these statistical facts.

Underlying Limbaugh's distortion lurks an even more serious logical error. Even if it had been factually accurate, his correlation of Democrats' control of Congress with gas-price escalation violates a basic rule of logical deduction. This fallacy has been known since antiquity as "post hoc ergo propter hoc" ("after this, because of this")

Primitives perpetuate superstitions via the post-hoc fallacy. During a drought, when it finally rains after the tribe stages 10 futile rain dances, the Indians are convinced that the eleventh dance caused rain. Such superstitions endure for centuries, even millennia. They are congenial to humankind's natural mental inertia. Logical thinking is as unnatural as the ballet.

Limbaugh is our most strident spokesman for moral and intellectual primitives who reason like savages. He, Sean Hannity, and their fellow talk-show hosts exploit a whole panoply of logical fallacies — the slippery slope, strawmen, red herrings, single-entry bookkeeping, circular reasoning, and heads-I-win-tails-you-lose. These are powerful, effective weapons for deceiving gullible mass audiences.

There is an obvious explanation for the rise in gas prices. With the rapid rise in oil demand from burgeoning industrial giants like China and India, oil economics collided with the law of supply and demand. In strict accordance with that law, oil prices skyrocketed with surging demand.

This explanation won't satisfy conspiracy theorists, who single out oil companies as uniquely satanic price-gouging monsters. Hedge-fund managers, speculating in futures markets, are probably the worst villains exploiting the situation to drive up oil prices above the supply-demand equilibrium price. But few in Limbaugh's audience know what a hedge fund is.

The catechism model

Besides the panoply of secular fallacies available to ideologues, there are religious fallacies. The transfer of religious bigotry into political bigotry is exhibited by two Catholic talk-show hosts, Bill O'Reilly and Sean Hannity. They have adapted the kindergarten style of the catechism's Q-and-A method of religious instruction to complex political problems, with predictably ridiculous results.

As a Catholic-raised child, I vividly recall this deadly nun-administered indoctrination. The catechism tests memory, not comprehension. You pass the test by parroting the precise prescribed answer to each question with a verbatim response; no variations from the text are allowed. As it does so well in stultifying thought in religious matters, the catechism technique stultifies thought in politics as well.

For those ignorant of the catechism Q-and-A method of indoctrination, a sample illustration will reveal its demeaning technique. To the question, "Why must every human being die?", here is the prescribed answer: "We must all die because we have all sinned in Adam. Saint Paul tells us, 'Sin entered the world through one man (i.e., Adam), and through sin, death' [Romans: 5-12]." As a child of five, I questioned the doctrine of Original Sin as unjust. It rejects the concept of individual responsibility. Its primitive roots lie deep in prehistory, when moral responsibility was

tribal, not individual. It's the mindless concept behind the feud ––
the senseless violence of the Montagues and the Capulets, or the
hillbilly feud between the Hatfields and McCoys. The catechism
forbids independent thought on this issue. You either accept it, or
risk spending an eternity in hell for your skepticism.

Transferred to the domain of politics, the catechism model
is equally stultifying. Talk-show host, Bill O'Reilly, dupes his
credulous audience with the catechism technique. For virtually
every political issue, O'Reilly has a brief, formalized Q-and-A
that demonstrates for all eternity the absolute truth of his political
philosophy. For one example, he defends the War on Drugs with
an anecdote about San Francisco's marijuana addicts allegedly
applying for medicinal drugs and then selling them on the street
at great profit. He doesn't tell you that the drug war itself, by
criminalizing drug use, is what sustains exorbitant illegal drug
prices. About the manifold evils associated with this mindless
metaphorical war –– widespread police corruption; diversion
of enforcement resources from more serious crimes; the idiotic
sentences for drug possession, sometimes exceeding those for rape
and other violent crimes; exemption of the most socially destructive
drug, alcohol, from the illegal substances, etc. –– O'Reilly has
nothing to say.

Applied to the Iraq war, the catechism process featured
this question by Hannity: "Is the world better off without
Saddam Hussein in power? Answer yes or no." Any attempt to
introduce complicating factors into the discussion drew Hannity's
interruption, "Just answer the question!" Any criticism of Bush's
war policy –– the demented fantasy behind its conception, the
gigantic strategic blunders in its execution, the priority of political
considerations over military objectives –– were drowned out with
the charge that the critic wished Saddam Hussein back in power.

Ideological gridlock

Though less adamant than politically reactionary ideologues,
liberal ideologues, too, have their irrational hangups. Nearly half

a century ago, in 1965, one of that rare breed of intellectually talented politicians, the late Senator Daniel Patrick Moynihan (D, NY) published a prescient study warning about the problem of black teenage pregnancy, which was increasing at enormous rates. Between 1960 and 2000, the black illegitimacy rate nearly tripled. In the worst-afflicted ghettos, illegitimacy approached 90 percent, and it now averages nearly 70 percent, more than four times its 1950 rate.

Since Moynihan's early data about black families' disintegration, the devastating social, political, and economic consequences of out-of-wedlock teenage pregnancy have been voluminously documented. Children born to poor teenage black mothers are disproportionately doomed to lives of criminality. While the white teenage crime rate held constant through the 2000s' decade, the black rate rose some 40 percent, to double the white rate. The prevalence of ghetto poverty assures extraordinarily high unemployment rates among children born to single teenage mothers, especially black mothers, the vast majority of whom are high-school dropouts. Children of high-school dropouts tend also tend to dropout. Parental academic interests and competence are, by far, the prime determinants of children's educational success. Unemployment and criminality are merely the worst aspects of ghetto children's social maladies.

As a reward for his prescient warning, Moynihan was vilified by liberal academics, called a racist for "blaming the victim." Liberal ideologues continued to oppose all effective efforts to turn things around. Moynihan's proposal to "make the daddies pay" got nowhere. The majority of irresponsibly breeding fathers are not identified, and, even if identified, are seldom forced to take responsibility for their acts — notably by paying child support. Measures requiring the mothers to identify fathers are rejected by liberal ideologues. And a recent report reveals another potent source of illegitimacy. Ghetto gang members seek the status achieved by promiscuous fatherhood, impregnating as many girls as possible to become known as a "big man." Black teenage girls told frequent stories of ghetto-dwelling males forcing them into unwanted pregnancies.

Some states have attempted to reduce the attraction of additional benefits to welfare mothers bearing additional children. In 1993, New Jersey enacted a law cutting off welfare benefits for additional children. Five years later, the welfare-mother birth rate had fallen by 31 percent, but some insisted that the rate was unaffected by the cutoff. The ACLU sued to repeal the law, and a liberal ideologue declared, "Government instructors have no business . . . telling mothers how many children to have." The New Jersey law (followed by other states) was enacted only after the welfare system was producing 32-year-old grandmothers. Teenage children exploited the welfare system by bearing babies as a means of qualifying for their own taxpayer-supported welfare apartments. In short, liberal ideology fostered a social policy combining total freedom with total publicly subsidized irresponsibility. Even the rights of crack-addicted mothers to spread ineffable suffering by bearing brain-damaged babies doomed to subnormal, dependent lives were deemed absolute. Efforts to prevent these tragedies were not only "politically incorrect," but viewed by extremists as revivals of Hitler's genocide.

Liberal ideologues press a similarly irrational case in their view of the white-black educational gap. Instead of a consequence of irresponsible breeding, manifest in the tremendous educational problems of black children born to poor single teenage mothers, some liberals see this problem as a civil rights issue, like the 1960s' legislation forcing racist Southerners to allow blacks to vote! In a book entitled, *The Black-White Achievement Gap: Why Closing It Is the Greatest Civil Rights Issue of our Time,* the book jacket contains this statement: "Unlike segregation, slavery, and discrimination, all . . . imposed intentionally by a racist society, no one is forcing this barrier to exist — yet it persists. And it has become the greatest civil rights issue of our time."

The book admits that blacks bear some responsibility for their generally poor academic performance — notably in calling academic success "behaving like whitey." But it ignores the educational effects of rampant illegitimacy. Omission of this overwhelmingly important factor can't be justified by merely focusing on schools' quality. Even the best teachers can't overcome the huge disadvantages of children deprived of concerned, responsible parents capable of encouraging their educational performance. Even where the teachers have been a demonstrable disaster, as in Washington, D.C., the black community appears to consider it more important to protect incompetent teachers' jobs than to improve their children's education. They effectively voted out a school chancellor, Michele Rhee, who had mounted a huge effort at improving teacher quality.

Logic is unnatural

Far from being exceptional, ideologues represent the dominant mode of thinking throughout history and prehistory. Logical, scientifically based reasoning is profoundly unnatural, a psychological barrier surmounted only by the astonishing ancient Greeks and resurrected after the Dark Ages by European Renaissance thinkers. Superstition is perpetuated by experience, through traditional fallacies embedded deep in our psyches. An incident reported in that remarkably readable and informative book, Francis Parkman's *The Oregon Trail*, shows how naturally reinforcing fear and superstition promote the post-hoc-ergo-propter-hoc fallacy. As a guest of a Sioux Indian tribe, in summer 1846, Parkman heard an old brave exclaim, "The thunder is bad; he killed my brother." Prodded for an explanation, the old brave remained stubbornly silent, possibly for fear of arousing the vengeful spirit of the thunder. Some time later, however, Parkman got the desired explanation. The thunder's victim, it seems, had belonged to a tribal association with the exclusive right to fight thunder. Whenever an undesired thunderstorm threatened, these thunder fighters would rush out to confront the offending cloud. Armed with bows and arrows, guns, a magic drum, and a whistle made from an eagle's wingbone, they would attempt to frighten the cloud away with an unholy racket, a cacophonous medley of war whoops, whistles, and drum beatings.

One afternoon, as a heavy black cloud rose over a hilltop, the thunder fighters climbed to the hilltop to challenge it. In Parkman's words, "...the undaunted thunder, refusing to be terrified, darted out a bright flash, which struck one of the party dead as he was in the very act of shaking his long iron-pointed lance against it. The rest scattered and ran yelling in an ecstasy of superstitious terror back to their lodges."

With our superior scientific knowledge, we moderns know why the Sioux thunder fighter was electrocuted. Lightning is a giant atmospheric electric spark connecting a negatively charged cloud bottom with the positively charged earth. The lightning's victim invited his death by brandishing his iron-pointed lance at the negatively charged cloud. He became a human lightning rod, attracting the fatal electric discharge. An informed, civilized man would know that such thunder-fighting tactics were suicidal.

But imagine trying to explain this process to the terrified Indians. Far from inspiring doubt about the thunder's maleficent intentions, their comrade's death dramatically confirmed their superstitious fears. It was, in fact, a classic case of psychological reinforcement. The Indians' world teemed with spirits; even a demon-inhabited stone could assert its evil intentions — by, for example, tripping a warrior. What, then, could be more reasonable than the thunder's wreaking vengeance on its enemy?

Science tells us that primitive thinking is natural. Xenophobia is evidently a natural evolutionary response to outsiders. At a basic level, we are wired to distrust strangers, according to University of Massachusetts researchers. Prejudice may well have evolutionary roots, developed as a quick, crude defense mechanism for early humans. Fear is apparently processed in two separate brain circuits. One reaction, in the primitive brain stem, occurs reflexively in the subconscious. The other, slower developing reaction, occurs in the cerebral cortex, where thoughts are rationally processed. Primitive minds are easily led astray by demagogic appeals to fear and paranoia.

Judged by the stupefyingly mindless Republican presidential primary debates of 2011-2012, a substantial portion of the American public has not risen far above the Sioux Indians hosting Francis Parkman. Not to denounce global warming science as a hoax would be political suicide for a Republican presidential candidate. Unequivocal agreement with the Theory of Evolution would jeopardize a Republican candidates' chances in a primary election. Polls show that Americans generally, Republicans more so, and Fox News viewers still more so believe that President Obama is a foreign-born Muslim, illegally elected President. As an equally absurd proof of their credulity, in October, 2003, two-thirds of Fox News viewers believed Vice President Cheney's cynically fabricated lie that Saddam Hussein had initiated the 9/11 attacks.

The Southern factor

Anti-scientific beliefs distinguish the United States from other industrially advanced nations, and the geographic core of this virulent anti-intellectualism is the Southern Bible Belt. There is plenty of illogical thinking throughout this nation, but in the Bible Belt anti-scientific thought has its deepest roots. This tradition thrives on simple-minded symbols –– the Confederate flag, Ten-Commandment courthouse displays, public school prayer. It preserves primitive attitudes through generations, like boulders trapped in glacial till. Comparing the civilization of New England ("a beacon lit upon a hill") with the benighted culture of the American South, the perceptive French historian, Alexis de Tocqueville, traced the South's decadent traditions back to the mother country's emigrants.

> *"The men sent to Virginia were seekers of gold, adventurers without resources and without character, whose turbulent and restless spirit endangered the infant colony, and rendered its progress uncertain....No lofty conceptions,*

no intellectual system, directed the foundation of these new settlements. The colony was scarcely established when slavery was introduced, and this was the main circumstance which has exercised so prodigious an influence on the character, the laws, and all the future prospects of the South.

Slavery...dishonors labor; it introduces idleness into society, and with idleness, ignorance and pride, luxury and distress. It enervates the powers of the mind, and benumbs the activity of man.

The roots of Appalachia's backward, anti-intellectual, poverty-perpetuating culture extend back to the impoverished British borderlands that exported these emigrants to America. These poor Scottish-Irish-English immigrants came from a culture of violence, indolence, and illiteracy. They made a stark contrast with the literate, pacific, communitarian East Anglicans who settled Massachusetts. These immigrants brought their debased culture with them. They perpetuate this culture through the natural inertia that keeps primitive societies in their ruts and draws advanced societies down unless they work at progress. From parents to children, cultural traditions perpetuate themselves through hapless generations. And the more primitive these traditions are, the more difficult it is to eradicate them.

These conclusions are buttressed by the great historian Richard Hofstadter. In *Anti-Intellectualism in American Life*, Hofstadter quotes an Anglican minister, Reverend Charles Woodmason, who traveled in the Carolina territory in the late colonial era, just prior to the revolution. Rev. Woodmason left a squalid depiction of savage backwoods life. Unlike English commoners, the American backwoodsmen bragged about their illiteracy. According to Rev.

Woodmason, "...these people despise knowledge, and instead of honouring a learned Person, or any man of Wit and Knowledge, be it in the Arts, Sciences, or languages, they despise and ill treat them. And this Spirit prevails even among the principals of this province."

The rough texture may have worn smoother in the intervening centuries, but this colonial-era depiction of the South still retains its essential validity.

The irony, of course, is the incredible political success achieved by the resurgent South after its Civil War defeat and long-endured economic eclipse by the Northern states. Some years ago, there was a jovial saying, "Hang onto your Confederate money, boys, the South will rise again." Confederate money never regained its original value. But with the triumph of the Republican-fundamentalist Party, the South did rise again.

Exhortation trumps education

In a critically important area requiring education —— i.e., sex education —— conservatives are AWOL. Their misnamed abstinence-only sex education is the very denial of education, for it omits the means —— i.e., contraception —— by which teenagers could avoid pregnancy as a consequence of sexual encounters. Abstinence-only sex education is merely anti-sex exhortation. Its futility is dramatically demonstrated in Bible-Belt states Mississippi and Texas, where teenage pregnancies exceed France's by a factor of 3 and Canada's by 4.

Conservative obstinacy in defending abstinence-only exhortation was dramatically illustrated by Sarah Palin's refusal to admit that failure despite the blatant example of her daughter Bristol's illegitimate pregnancy. At the 2008 Republican National Convention, this failure was transmogrified into a success. The McCain-Palin ticket diverted attention from the abstinence-only exhortation to the anti-abortion message promoted by Bristol's decision to bear the baby. It was a classic illustration of conservative propagandists' tactic of changing the subject as a means of avoiding rational debate.

Between them, liberal and conservative ideologues assure the persistence of the status quo on black illegitimacy. Like other issues where public discussion is suppressed by political correctness or immovable ideological opposition, teenage pregnancy and its dismal consequences are a largely lost cause, limited to incremental, rather than fundamental, reform. Conservatives back policies that promote the birth of unwanted black children, and liberals back policies that indulge unwanted pregnancies. What at best is an immensely difficult problem ideologues make impossible. Recent slight reductions in illegitimacy are attributable almost solely to teenagers' increased use of contraception. And conservatives are bitterly opposed to contraception as well as abortion.

At the heart of reactionary Southern politics is the persistence of primitive religion, the anti-scientific evangelical Christianity that dominates the Bible Belt. Aspiring Republican presidential candidates — notably, Texas Governor Rick Perry — exemplified this proclivity. When Governor Perry suggested that God may have caused the devastating 2010 Gulf of Mexico oil spill, ostensibly as punishment for some unspecified national evil, he was expressing primitive religion's core belief: God maintains intimate control over our lives and must be propitiated for the tribe to prosper. Primitive religion is tribal rather than personal. Hence the Republican insistence that candidates must constantly proclaim their piety, as they did in primitive, ancient societies, where priests and kings united as the people's masters.

At the Tea Party's geographical core, the Southern Bible Belt exhibits the cynical exploitation of poor whites by their greedy superiors, a long tradition in this benighted region. During the Civil War, a man owning 20 or more slaves was exempt from military service. It was the millions of non-slaveowning whites who were expected to fight for their slaveholding social superiors. Today's exploiters of poor Southern whites are still their social superiors. The Koch Brothers, casino magnate Sheldon Adelson, and other multibillionaires have convinced these gullible masses that their self interest lies in reducing the taxes and widening the huge wealth gap that isolates them from their exploiters.

Propaganda payoff

Intimately associated with the logical fallacies characteristic of ideological thinking is gross ignorance. Political ignorance is appalling in the general population, but among the Republican Party's "fair-and-balanced" Fox News viewers it goes beyond appalling. Here are the results of a September, 2009, National Public Radio poll:

- 75 percent of Fox News viewers (vs. 45 percent of Americans generally), believe that health-care reform legislation allows the federal government to dictate end-of-life decisions. (This is the Sarah Palin "death-panel" myth.)
- 41 percent believed, falsely, that their taxes increased since Obama became President.
- 63 percent believed that Obama was not born in the U.S.
- 46 percent believed that Obama is a Muslim

An earlier poll (October, 2003) revealed that two-thirds of Fox News viewers believed Dick Cheney's lie: "The U.S. had clear evidence in Iraq that Saddam Hussein was working with the Al Qaeda terrorist organization." Only 23 percent (one-third as many) NPR radio listeners believed that cynically fabricated falsehood.

Republicans as a whole are nearly as gullible as Fox News viewers. In early 2011, a Republican majority, 51 percent, believed that Obama was foreign born; only 28 percent believed that he was born in the U.S. This despite the publication of his birth certificate.

The difficulty of thinking logically

Researchers have demonstrated the vast difficulty of changing minds through presentation of facts contradicting ideological beliefs. Emotions can easily overpower logic. Logical thinking is, at best, extremely difficult. My logic textbook gives an example of a false syllogism, which nonetheless appears generally valid.

All radicals are foreign born; no patriotic citizen is a radical; therefore no patriotic citizen is foreign born.

Here is a precisely parallel syllogism, but one easily refuted:

All triangles are plane figures; no squares are triangles; therefore no squares are plane figures.

Here's the explanation why the first syllogism is erroneous: Nothing in the two premises denies that a patriotic citizen can be foreign born.

In the ensuing chapters, I discuss the factual omissions and distortions and the voluminous perversions of logical exploited chiefly by so-called political conservatives to confuse huge segments of the public.

CHAPTER 2

Newspeak, 21st-Century Style

"But 'glory' doesn't mean a 'nice knockdown argument,'" Alice objected.

"When I use a word," Humpty Dumpty said, "it means just what I choose it to mean — neither more nor less."

Lewis Carroll

"My education message will resignate among all parents."

"A tax cut is really one of the anecdotes to coming out of an economic illness."

former President George W. Bush

Political ideologues' assault on scientific thinking begins with perversion of language. This perversion is epitomized by the use of "conservative" for the accurate word, "reactionary." According to standard dictionary definitions, a "conservative" is disposed to preserve existing conditions and institutions, whereas a "reactionary" wants to return to a "former or less advanced condition."

The contemporary Republican Party's goals are clearly reactionary. A comparison of current Republican ideology with Theodore Roosevelt's shows how, in the 21st century, Republicans urge us to retreat back through the 20th century into the 19th-century robber barons' politics. Theodore Roosevelt proposed inheritance taxes when John D. Rockefeller, J.P. Morgan, Jay Gould, and other rich malefactors were consolidating their economic power and amassing huge fortunes. Today's Republicans want to abolish the inheritance tax. TR sponsored anti-trust legislation designed to limit the robber barons' concentrated power. Contemporary Republicans take the bankers' and other corporate campaign contributions and do their bidding, opposing all regulatory reform. TR introduced environmental legislation to conservative natural resources. Republican presidential candidates either want to abolish the Environmental Protection Agency or to vastly curtail its enforcement actions. Republicans side with industry's demand that taxpayers pay for cleaning up industry's toxic wastes. Even more significant as an indication of his commitment to scientific reasoning, TR championed the theory of evolution in the 1880s, when the scientific community itself was still adapting to the revolutionary new science. More than a century later, former President George W. Bush said the jury was still out on evolution. Republican presidential candidate Rick Perry went even further, advocating the teaching of Creationism in biology class. Belief in global-warming science is banned to any serious Republican presidential candidate. Republican efforts to kill the long enfeebled labor-union movement indicate an ideological dedication to reversing political progress.

Logic v. emotion

Shakespeare's famous maxim, "A rose by any other name would smell as sweet," is demonstrably false. Republicans proved Shakespeare wrong with a long campaign to sway public opinion on the alleged immorality of inheritance taxes. Correctly known either as estate or inheritance tax, this tax is widely accepted by the public as moral and reasonable. As previously noted, that was TR's view. When Republicans decided to substitute the dysphemistic phrase, "death tax," however, the public turned against the tax.

It took an elaborate propaganda campaign to effect this changed attitude. Forever seeking to cut taxes for the rich, Republicans conducted focus-group studies to find out how to build popular consensus for abolishing the estate tax. Republican language guru, Frank Luntz, sought to find out which tax focus-group participants would most want to abolish: estate, inheritance, or "death" taxes. Anyone with elementary intelligence would have recognized the logical equivalence of these three taxes. But the focus group members lacked even this slight perspicacity. Though obviously logically equivalent, these terms were anything but emotionally equivalent. By a large margin, a "death" tax was collectively deemed the most onerous. In ensuing discussion following the vote, group members indignantly vented about the death tax's injustice. (You work all your life, and government bureaucrats take your money away at the end.) Focus-group participants had no idea about how few estates were taxed. (At the time it was roughly 1 percent and has currently shrunk to about 0.3 percent, to couples whose estates exceed $7 million.) But even questioned about whether Bill Gates's heirs should pay tax on a fortune of $50 billion or so at the time, focus-group members still opposed even a 1 percent tax.

Republican propagandists instituted a campaign to purge references to "estate" or "inheritance" taxes in favor of the emotion-laden "death" tax. *The Wall Street Journal* adheres faithfully to this rule. Business groups and Republican congressmen, led by former House Speaker Newt Gingrich, fined anyone a dollar for calling the estate tax by its honest name. Anything other than "death" tax was heresy.

The energetic Luntz has other advice for politicians who prey on Americans' emotional reactions to language. When you want to intensify opposition, you say "Washington" or "IRS." When you want to bolster support, you say "Department of Defense" instead of "Pentagon," "tax relief instead of "tax cuts," and "climate change" instead of "global warming."

In a ludicrous attempt to evade the global-warming issue, Virginia state legislator Chris Stolle convinced his colleagues to reject the phrase "sea-level rise," a perfectly accurate description of the 14.5-in. increase in sea-level elevation along the state's southern coast. Instead of what Representative Stolle called a "left-wing term," the Virginia legislator substituted the phrase "recurrent coastal flooding," predicted to increase because of a projected 27-in. sea-level rise by 2200.

Luntz scored even bigger with his advice to attack Democratic health reform with the phrase "government takeover of health care." Republicans took this advice and won a huge propaganda victory. Appearing on Meet the Press, then House Minority Leader John Boehner referred to Obama's plan five times as a "government takeover." without once being challenged. Polls demonstrated the success of the distorted propaganda. Obama's health plan relies on private insurance and market pricing, albeit with government regulation. PolitiFact.com, a fact-checking agency of the Petersburg Times, awarded Luntz with its 2010 prize for "lie of the year." Nonetheless, a Bloomberg poll recorded 53 percent convinced that "Obamacare" was a government takeover. Gallup reported that 65 percent thought it expanded government't role "too much." And Gallup later reported that 10 percent considered "government involvement in Health care" our worst problem, worse than health-care cost of lack of access. A decade earlier only 1 percent held this view.

"Death panels" and other horrors

Creating public antipathy to health-care reform has been perhaps the Republicans' chief success through the obfuscating strategy of horrifying the populace with deceptive words and phrases. President Obama's effort to provide end-of-life counseling in health-care regulations resurrected the charge of "death panels." At that time there were real death panels in the U.S. Arizona Governor Jan Brewer instituted a real death panel, denying dying patients access to bone-marrow and other transplants essential to their survival. This genuine death panel elicited a deafening silence from Sarah Palin and her admirers. But federal end-of-life counseling, with no provision for denying necessary treatment, they called "pulling the plug on grandma."

Palin initiated her original 2009 death-panel charge ferociously. "The America I know and love is not one in which my parents or my baby with Down syndrome will have to stand in front of Obama's 'death panel' so his bureaucrats can decide . . . whether they are worthy of health care."

This is a big, black lie. There was nothing remotely resembling Palin's death-panel fabrication in the health-care bill, HR3200. It merely established advance-care planning –– doctor-patient consultation about medical procedures desired, or rejected, by the patient –– e.g., whether a patient wants mechanical breathing aid if he is permanently comatose. This patient-doctor consultation would inform patients about living wills and durable power of attorney.

Advanced medical planning is desperately needed to control escalating medical costs. Only some 15 percent of Americans have made living wills, stating what they want if physically incapacitated and thus unable to express their desires. Not knowing a patient's desires, doctors and hospitals overwhelmingly opt for maximum treatment, regardless of prognosis and cost. Millions of Americans die after long, hopeless struggles –– futile, painwracked battles against cancer, organ failure, and other old-age debilities. Modern medical technology can readily prolong "life" into the braindead, vegetative state. Doctor-patient consultation allows patients to refuse this dismal destiny.

By some estimates, the U.S. could save $700 billion annually, 30 percent of our total national health-care bill, if hospitals and doctors could refrain from useless medical care. But there are powerful incentives promoting useless care –– defensive medicine to avoid frivolous malpractice lawsuits, plus the monetary incentive of higher hospital and doctor payments.

Those who defend prolongation of doomed aged lives, denouncing health-care rationing and death panels, should be more incensed at Governor Brewer's death panels for thirty-year olds. But demagogues gain more through fear mongering about imaginary evils than by confronting real ones.

Obliterating meaning

The corruption of political language has entered the Newspeak stage prophesied by George Orwell in *Nineteen-Eighty-Four*. Like Big Brother's INGSOC slogans –– "War Is Peace; Freedom is Slavery; Ignorance is Strength" –– contemporary propaganda goes far beyond innuendo, euphemism, dysphemism, mangled metaphors, false statistics, slippery-slope fallacy, and other traditional techniques of obfuscation. Today's political propagandists aim at the annihilation of meaning.

Absolute moralists are prominent among those assaulting the language. Anti-abortionists are major culprits. Their endlessly repeated mantra, "Abortion is murder," insults public intelligence. "Murder" is a legal term, defined in my dictionary as "the unlawful killing of another human being with malice aforethought." Since it is legal, abortion, ipso facto, cannot be murder. No intensity of moral conviction can alter this simple fact. You can argue that abortion should be outlawed and thus classified as murder. But you can't rationally argue that it *is* murder.

As someone constantly struggling for the precise word to convey meaning, I am perpetually disgusted with politicians' word choices solely for their emotional impact. Confronted with a barbarous atrocity, they can't resist the temptation to label it with some emotionally laden epithet, no matter how inappropriate.

This proclivity for substituting moral outrage for accurate thought was evident in President George W. Bush's initial reaction to the 9/11 attacks. Soon after the terrorists had traded their 19 lives for nearly 3,000 American lives, President Bush reacted with an idiotic response. He called the suicide terrorists "cowards."

This ludicrous misuse of language is a recent phenomenon. No one, to my knowledge, ever called the World War II Japanese kamikaze pilots cowards when they sacrificed their lives diving their bomb-laden planes onto the decks of American warships. There was plenty of verbal distortion during World War II. But even the worst demagogues generally retained some connection between words and meaning.

Labeling suicide terrorists cowards is preposterous. Cowardice is a shrinking from physical pain or danger. How can anyone seriously apply this word to people who sacrifice their lives for their cause? There are a host of appropriate epithets for suicide terrorists: barbarous, savage, fanatical, paranoid, psychopathic, delusional. But suicide-committing terrorists are the very opposite of cowardly. Using such a ludicrously mangled word to express disgust precludes all hope of understanding their motivation.

When you descend to this primitive level of thought, you lose all hope of formulating a rational foreign policy. Simply calling the terrorists enemies of freedom, without the slightest effort to understand their motives, is a useless, wheel-spinning exercise. Thinking is much harder work than moralizing. It also has another political disadvantage. Thinking gets you much less political mileage than mindless demagoguery, *pandering* to mass fear and ignorance.

Euphemism and dysphemism

Moral passion, the obvious source of much verbal abuse, is a less common source of corrupt language than the cynical intellectual dishonesty that characterizes contemporary politics.

Euphemism and dysphemism are the major techniques of today's political propagandists. (As brief illustrative definitions, "pass away" is a euphemism, "croak" a dysphemism for the conventionally neutral word, "die.")

As wars invariably do, the Iraq War spawned euphemisms constructed to blur the stark realities. "Collateral damage" is the phrase used to disguise the facts about thousands of civilian maimings and deaths in pursuit of Iraqi terrorists. "Enhanced interrogation techniques" (EIT to Bush insiders) is the phrase used to evade charges of inflicting torture.

Political corruption spawns self-serving phraseology. "Constituent service," a deceptive euphemism evidently still in use, was exploited a quarter century ago by the notorious Keating Five (which included Senator John McCain) in their desperate defense of their sellout to the savings-and-loan crook, Charles Keating. In an institutional defense labeled a "whitewash" by *The Washington Post* and a "farce" by *The New York Times*, the Senate Ethics Committee defended the "constituent services" provided by the Keating Five to their financial contributors. Keating had paid his five Senatorial minions well over $1 million to intimidate federal regulators vainly attempting to save taxpayers $2.5 billion attributable to Keating's reckless, dishonest policies. A "constituent" is "a voter in a district represented by an elected official." Thus Keating could not have been a "constituent" of five U.S. Senators representing four different states. Was the Senate Ethics Committee really unable to distinguish between a constituent and a contributor? The Keating Five served their constituents, the taxpaying victims of the savings-and-loan fiasco perpetrated by Charles Keating and his fellow thieves, by presenting them with immensely higher tax bills required to pay for the savings-and-loan bailout's roughly $250-billion cost. But in the corrupt language of Washington politics, this constituent disservice was defended as constituent service.

For the most humorous political euphemism, we must turn to *The Wall Street Journal's* editorial page. Defending former Senator Bob Packwood, forced to resign in 1995 after his exposure as the Senate's most notorious sex harasser, the *Journal* described this legislative Lothario's prolific lying with the phrase, "factually flexible." We can only speculate about the provenance of this weird metaphor, obviously intended to lend a friend a little leeway in bending, twisting, and stretching the truth. Commenting about its political enemies, however, the *Journal* has no hesitance in using the appropriate word *liar*. And in the editorial defending Senator Packwood, it referred to to Packwood's critics as "an activist mob" and the hearings into his misdeeds as an "exorcism."

Liberals as well as conservatives have their favorite euphemisms. To *The New York Times*, the accurate term "illegal alien" is evidently taboo. Illegal aliens in *Times* editorials are "undocumented aliens," a term that obscures the harsh reality. It is obviously more compassionate to refer to undocumented aliens rather than illegal aliens, but it doesn't help the understanding. But ideologues appear always willing to sacrifice truth to expedience. If you believe in an open-borders immigration policy, it is easier to defend your ideology with emotion-based words than with honest words. Unfortunately, it is also probably more effective.

Painting things black

Whereas euphemism blurs stark details with verbal fog, transforming skullduggery into innocuous, even virtuous action, dysphemism does just the reverse. Through devious use of dysphemism, political propagandists create monstrous exaggerations and turn truth and falsehood inside out. Like the entertainment industry exploiting its dominating power to extol its virtues ("There're no people like show people"), politicians and their propagandists employ dysphemisms to extol politicians' virtues.

This proclivity for ludicrous exaggeration is illustrated by use of the word, "death," as a synonym for electoral defeat. *Wall Street Journal* reporter Gerald Seib attributes the "timidity" of Republican congressmen in early 1997 to a "brush with death" in the 1996 elections. When Robert Dole resigned from the U.S. Senate to run for President, Senator Phil Gramm praised this allegedly courageous gamble as "a choice between victory or death." In this context, "death," of course, meant the horrors of removal from public office and banishment to the Outer Darkness of a sinecure with a Washington law firm, where Dole made millions as a super lobbyist. For Senator Gramm, a draft-dodging supporter of the Vietnam War, who never saw military service, such a gamble might actually appear courageous. But to Senator Dole, who faced literal death on the Italian front in World War II and was wounded there, praise for this mock political heroism must have seemed sick. So does a recent denunciation of biennial elections for subjecting U.S. Representatives to the continual "risk of martyrdom." The author of that phrase believes that the Constitution's authors erred in designing an electoral system that keeps political heat on House members.

This straight-faced equating of electoral defeat with death is ludicrous for two reasons. Politicians constantly inform us that public service for such talented persons as themselves constitutes an enormous personal sacrifice. They could make multiples of their modest congressional salaries in the private sector — or so they tell us. The death-equated horror of electoral defeat thus entails no financial sacrifice at all — in fact, just the opposite.

The defeat-equals-death thesis becomes even more ludicrous when politics is compared with vocations for which death is not a preposterous metaphor, but a stark, chronic reality. We ask policemen to risk death in high-speed auto chases and shootouts with desperate criminals. We ask firemen to risk death rescuing people trapped in burning buildings. Servicemen routinely risk death in military missions, even training exercises. To anyone with a modicum of mental and emotional balance, the equation of electoral defeat with death is sentimental nonsense.

Metaphorical wars

Declarations of war on terrorism, poverty, Christmas and the West all portray the metaphorical political wars facilitated by the war on language. An imaginary War on Christmas thrived during the Bush years, but has since receded as its ludicrous exaggerations became ever more obvious. Several years ago, Fox News author John Gibson's book, *The War on Christmas: How the Liberal Plot to Ban the Sacred Christian Holiday Is Worse Than You Thought*, revealed this preposterous myth in its hysterically exaggerated title. Fox New's demagogic prostitutes —— notably, Bill O'Reilly —— defend Christian martyrs against their pagan tormentors. The holiday's survival testifies to the successful crusade against the secular infidels, ignominiously thwarted in their efforts to destroy it. *New York Times* columnist Frank Rich had it more accurately assessed: ". . . there was no war on Christmas, but rather a burgeoning myth about a war on Christmas."

Injustice to the rich, but suffering recipients of federal subsidies spawned another spurious metaphorical war —— "War on the West." It was allegedly waged by President Bill Clinton's Interior Secretary, Bruce Babbitt, in the mid-1990s. This bombastic phrase is an all-purpose charge against feeble efforts not to abolish, but merely to reduce the huge taxpayer-financed subsidies traditionally lavished upon western ranchers, mining operators, and farmers.

Federal mining legislation is an especially generous taxpayer giveaway, with the trivial federal payments set by an ancient 1872 law that levies trivial mining fees. In addition to the subsidized beneficiaries, the chorus parroting this charge, "War on the West," comprises federal and state legislators who sedulously preach free market ideology, except, of course, when it benefits their campaign contributors.

"War on the West" is reminiscent of the rebel Southerners' verbal strategy when the narrow interests of a small minority of wealthy slaveholders exempted from military service masqueraded as a universal interest and sent several hundred thousand poor men to their deaths fighting for "the Southern way of life." In a similar way, "War on the West" falsely identifies the interests of a small minority of federally subsidized beneficiaries with the interests of an entire regional population.

"As proof that these absurd metaphorical wars are becoming ever more preposterous, we have an Alabama congressman's midsummer 2014 diatribe against President Obama's alleged "War on Whites."

Rewrite the dictionary

Contrasted with the subtler techniques of distorting language — euphemisms to soften harsh realities, dysphemisms to magnify or create mythical injustices, moral outrage to falsely frame an issue — there is also simple misuse of words. Rush Limbaugh is a notorious perpetrator. When critics of the Iraq War referred to the huge problem posed by the military occupation, Limbaugh simply denied that our military forces were occupying Iraq. As one of its many dictionary definitions, occupation includes this: "the seizure and control of an area by military forces, especially foreign territory." I can't imagine a more accurate concordance with that definition than our former occupation of Iraq. But you can't confuse Limbaugh with verbal facts. To Rush and his listeners we were not occupying Iraq.

Quagmire was another verboten word applied to Iraq. In my dictionary, its second (metaphorical) definition is "a situation from which extrication is very difficult." You might think that here was at least one small point on which anyone with the power of conscious thought could agree. But again, contending against politically reactionary ideologues, you get an argument. Even at the height of the Sunni-Shiite conflict and the continual terrorist attacks on our occupying troops, Iraq was no quagmire.

If Orwell were alive today, he would be appalled at the current development of Newspeak, but he would not be shocked. Orwell, after all, lived at a time when murderous attacks on native villages were called "pacification" and the Holocaust's ineffable horrors were shrouded in the verbal mist of "the final solution."

Our founding fathers, however, would be shocked. Imagine Jefferson, Madison, and Hamilton, fastidious artists in the nuances of language and elevated political discourse, confronting our congressmen's brazenly fraudulent claim that their out-of-state

31

campaign donors were their "constituents." Words are the tools of thought, and so long as we tolerate their willful mangling, we will never solve our most debilitating social and political problems. By allowing politically correct intimidation to censor candid analyses of illegitimacy with the reflexive charge of racism, we assure continuance of virtually stupefied impotence in confronting this socially destructive problem. And so long as our political reporters passively tolerate politicians' systematic corruption of language, we can count on the perpetuation of systemic political corruption.

CHAPTER 3

The Reversal-of-Proof Fallacy

"That Adam was formed of dirt procured in this spot is amply proven by the fact that in six thousand years no man has been able to prove that the dirt was not procured here whereof he was made."

Mark Twain
INNOCENTS ABROAD

Ever since the 1869 publication of *Innocents Abroad*, with its account of a visit to the Holy Land, Mark Twain's joke has entertained literature-loving Americans with his "proof" about the origin of Adam's dirt. Twain's joke, however, would have baffled the Bush administration's top officials. Vice President Dick Cheney habitually reversed the burden of proof. For one notorious example, take Cheney's response to the 9/11 Commission's 2004 report. Investigating Cheney's charge that Saddam Hussein was linked to Al Qaeda, and thus to the 9/11 attacks, the commission staff found no substantiating evidence. Cheney had claimed that Muhammed Atta, the suicide hijackers' leader, had met with an Iraqi spy in Prague prior to 9/11. Attempting to rebut the commission's doubts that this meeting had occurred, Cheney first admitted that Atta's Prague visit had never been proved. He then noted that it had never been refuted. Yes, and during his Holy Land visit, Mark Twain was standing at the exact spot where the Creator had scooped up the dirt from which Adam was sculpted. After all, as Twain accurately noted, in 6,000 years no one had proved that the dirt was *not* procured from the exact spot where he was standing. Cheney's evidence of Muhammed Atta's meeting with an Iraqi spy was logically identical to Twain's proof of Adam's origin. And this instance was not atypical of Cheney's intellectual modus operandi.

Former Defense Secretary Donald Rumsfeld was another prominent burden-of-proof reverser. Like many mediocre intellects, Rumsfeld considers himself extremely clever. Questioned about the Bush administration's failure to find weapons of mass destruction (WMDs) in Iraq, Rumsfeld triumphantly replied, "Absence of evidence is not evidence of absence." Translation: "Heads I win; tails you lose." It was not Rumsfeld's burden to prove the WMD thesis correct; it was critics' responsibility to prove him wrong. With its totalitarian secrecy and its cavalier attitude toward truth, the Bush Administration employed Looking-Glass logic that made it theoretically impossible to rebut its claims.

In an even more preposterous proof reversal, President Bush's first press secretary, Ari Fleischer, did his more prominent colleagues one better. "I think the burden is on those people who think he [i.e., Saddam Hussein] didn't have WMDs to tell the world where they are." Fleischer's demand makes convoluted logic convoluted squared. If, as Fleischer argues, skeptics bear the burden of proof of providing an alternative to an unproven assertion that they challenge as a condition of rejecting it, then we're in a world purged of logic.

Republicans reverse the burden of proof for their constantly parroted mantra: Tax cuts for the rich are essential for economic growth. Confronted with the voluminous evidence contradicting this thesis, the thriving economy when Bush 41 and Clinton raised these taxes, coupled with the dismal economy when Bush 43 cut them, Congressman and 2012 Republican vice presidential candidate, Paul Ryan, went beyond the usual reliance on repetition, with its implied burden-of-proof reversal, and challenged the idea that correlation is causation. It is true, of course, that correlation is not necessarily causation. But in this instance, Rep. Ryan went far beyond a denial that correlation equals causation. He was effectively arguing that *negative* correlation is causation. This is truly a remarkable logical discovery. If negative rather than positive correlation is causation, then black is white; white is black; up is down, and East is West. What we say is true is true, because we say it.

Beyond politics

Proof reversal is not limited to political ideologues. The worst perpetrator of medical fraud, claiming that he has demonstrated a link between autism and childhood vaccines for measles, mumps, and whooping cough, defended his fraudulent thesis with a burden-of-proof reversal. Former Dr. Andrew Wakefield somehow persuaded the British medical journal, *The Lancet*, to publish his "research" allegedly demonstrating the vaccine-autism link. More than a decade after the 1998 publication of this "research," *The Lancet's* editors learned of Wakefield's fraud. (On the basis of a dozen or so subjects, he arrived at his conclusion, which was encouraged by a huge conflict of interest. He was retained as a prospective expert witness testifying for plaintiffs' lawyers in lawsuits filed against the vaccine manufacturers.) As a consequence of his fraud, the UK Medical Council revoked Wakefield's medical license.

Here is his brazen defense: "Any medical professional, government official, or journalist who states the case is closed on whether vaccines cause autism is jumping to conclusions without the research to back it up." It's up to his opponents to conduct research proving his -- Wakefield's -- fraudulent research wrong!

Burden-of-proof reversal perpetuated the ludicrous "birther" issue, believed by an astonishing 45 percent of Republicans expressing their belief that President Obama was not a natural citizen as late as April, 2011 -- just before he produced his long-form birth certificate. (The long-form provided no relevant information not available on the short-form certificate, which had established Obama's citizenship two years earlier, but that was too subtle a point for the birthers.)

Here was an interesting case, as often happens, when the burden of proof reverses with the progress of the controversy. At the original challenge of his citizenship, the burden could reasonably be laid upon President Obama. But after he first produced his birth certificate, the burden shifted to his opponents. Their most fanatical advocates, of course, refused to accept this logic. Even after he produced the proof, the more fanatical birthers could invent new reasons for doubt. Donald Trump, the megalomaniacal financier who resurrected the issue in his farcical, presidential campaign', maintained a skeptical attitude and promised to continue his obviously spurious "investigation." Trump predictably never reported the investigation's results.

Stand up for nonsense

So-called "stand-your-ground" laws enacted in several, chiefly Southern states, create absurd proof reversals that corrupt the criminal justice system. Two notorious Florida cases, involving the killing of two black teenagers by white defendants, evidently allowed the two defendants to get away with murder. Prosecutors bore the burden of proof that the murder-charged defendants did not kill in self defense. In states lacking stand-your-ground laws, the burden of proof lies, of course, on defendants to prove their self-defense arguments.

In the first Florida case, the highly publicized Trayvon Martin killing in February, 2012, defendant George Zimmerman was exonerated despite his active pursuit of the unarmed black teenager, whom he erroneously suspected of thievery. In the second, so-called "loud-music" murder case, the defendant, Michael Dunn, won a mistrial when at least one juror found some reason to believe that his unarmed victim was, as Dunn claimed, armed with a shotgun. Dunn failed to claim that his victim was armed until a full day after the killing. These stand-your-ground laws are severe warnings against burden-of-proof reversals in the courts, whose criteria make them doubly difficult to pursue. (Dunn's conviction of attempted murder of three teenagers in a car into which he fired 10 bullets does not detract from the the injustice of his murder-trial failure.)

The Nixon precedent

The reversal-of-proof fallacy had precedents in the Nixon administration. In a *New Yorker* article, Senator William J. Fulbright described the logic of Cold War psychology during the Vietnam War.

"The truly remarkable thing about this Cold War psychology is the totally illogical transfer of the burden of proof from those who make charges to those who question them. In this frame of reference, Communists are guilty until proven innocent — or simply by definition. The Cold Warriors instead of having to say how they knew that Vietnam was part of a plan for the Communization of the world, so manipulated the terms of public discussion as to be able to demand that the skeptics prove that it was not. . . . We came to the ultimate illogic: War is the course of prudence and sobriety until the case for peace is proved under impossible rules of evidence — or until the enemy surrenders."

As Senator Fulbright eloquently argued in *The New Yorker*, the underlying explanation for widespread acceptance of Looking-Glass logic during the Cold War was fear. Just as Communist bogeymen inspired irrational fear in the Cold War era, so do misnamed "Islamofascists" inspire fear today. For the exploiters of fear, the current threat is always history's greatest. Before the Iraq War, the same Rightwing demagogues who rail about Islamofascists today compared Saddam Hussein to Hitler. Even the slightest knowledge about that third-rate thug would have deterred any rational person from such making such a preposterous charge. During the 1930s, Hitler created one of history's most formidable military machines. The 1940 German Blitzkrieg blasted its way through Belgium, Netherlands, and France, giving Hitler virtual control of the entire European continent. The Nazis did pose a unique threat to civilization. Hitler was a paranoid fanatic of incomparable ability to inspire his powerful nation's masses and enlist their support of his megalomaniacal dreams.

By contrast, Saddam Hussein was a pathetic, third-rate thug. Despite the Reagan Administration's continual military aid, he couldn't defeat Iran in his eight-year war with that fellow Muslim nation during the 1980s. While his physicists were stealing money supposedly appropriated for development of WMDs, Saddam was frivolously preoccupied with writing a novel. Comparing Saddam with Hitler was farcical.

Judicial Logic

Twain's joke about the authenticity-proof of Adam's dirt is serious logic for Supreme Court Justice Antonin Scalia as well as Dick Cheney. At a prayer breakfast at the Mississippi College law school, Justice Scalia denounced "secular intellectuals" who, without evidence, reject the Easter miracle of Jesus's post-crucifixion resurrection. It is irrational to reject miracles *a priori*, argued Scalia. "What is irrational to reject [is] . . . the possibility of miracles and the resurrection of Jesus Christ, which is precisely what the worldly wise do." Justice Scalia believes that skeptics bear the burden of proof in the question of Jesus's resurrection. It's not up to believers to prove that Jesus survived crucifixion and several days later ascended to heaven. It's up to skeptics to prove that he didn't! Justice Scalia never explained how you could prove that a supernatural event, allegedly occurring 2,000 years ago, never occurred. Turning the tables, we can ask how Scalia could prove that Mohammed, mounted on his favorite steed, didn't ascend to heaven from Jerusalem's Dome of the Rock 14 centuries ago.

The ultimate proof reverser

In the political world, Sean Hannity is an egregiously stubborn burden-of-proof reverser. Once he gets his teeth clamped on an ideologically comfortable proposition, Hannity develops a severe case of lockjaw. Long after the Terri Schiavo case had been settled, judicially and polemically, Hannity stuck by his original opinion that something was rotten in Florida. Even after medical research proved that Mrs. Schiavo had been braindead for 15 years, Hannity persisted in denying the medical facts. Backed by the opinion of Mark Fuhrmann, the Los Angeles police detective who committed spectacular perjury in the O.J. Simpson murder trial, Hannity parted with more rational colleagues, even Rush Limbaugh, who sensibly let the WMD subject drop.

Guilty Until Proven Innocent

My favorite political writer, George Orwell, opens his essay on Gandhi with a provocative asseveration: Saints should be judged guilty until proven innocent. When I first encountered this reversal of the innocent-until-proven-guilty criterion, I was astonished that Orwell would challenge this widely parroted maxim. A little reflection, however, should convince you that Orwell was onto something with this reversal of the judicial criterion.

When first promulgated by the Roman emperor Antoninus Pius in the Second century, innocent-until-proven-guilty reversed the normal legal rule prevalent in the ancient world (and carried through Europe's Dark and Middle Ages). There are, of course, sound reasons justifying this reversal. On one hand, it establishes some balance between the state's awesome power and the accused individual's lesser power to marshall evidence. More importantly, it recognizes the safeguards required in any civilized society to assure the truth of charges that can lead to a defendant's incarceration or, in capital cases, to execution. If an error is made, it should favor the freeing of the guilty over punishment of the innocent. That's fundamental to modern judicial philosophy.

So powerful is the appeal of this idea that it has been stretched far beyond its properly limited scope. The presumption that defendants in criminal trials should be deemed innocent until proven guilty is backed by centuries of bitter historical experience. It is essential to protect innocent victims from overzealous prosecutors. When a human being's life or liberty is at stake, civilized societies demand a high probability, verging on virtual certainty, that he is, in fact, guilty. If an error is made, it is better to free the guilty than to convict the innocent.

Politicians, however, have perverted the innocent-until-guilty principle, stretching it into an all-purpose defense in politically embarrassing situations. It has, in fact, become a smokescreen for all sorts of political chicanery. As a classic example, consider the 1989 Senate hearings on President George H.W. Bush's nominee, former Texas Senator John Tower, as Defense Secretary. Against the Tower nomination, there were well documented doubts about his sobriety and even graver doubts about his conflicts of interest. Within weeks following termination as chief U.S. arms negotiator, Tower was exploiting this experience as a "consultant" to Martin Marietta and other big military contractors. For vague services comprising little more than inside information, Tower received more than $1 million in fees. These conflicts aroused justifiable doubts that a nominee personally indebted to military contractors for past financial favors would diligently combat the perennial, multi-billion-dollar waste and fraud endemic to Pentagon procurement programs.

To Senator Alan Simpson (R, WY), however, Tower was a victim of overzealous prosecution. No court would have convicted Tower on the basis of the presented evidence, argued Simpson. He naturally failed to specify the hypothetical charge against Tower in this opaque analogy. But it's clear what he was suggesting with his demagogic innuendo. He was suggesting that Tower had a *right* to a job for which he had been nominated, and that to deny him that job was tantamount to a criminal conviction.

This is, of course, simplistic nonsense. Rejection of a presidential nominee is in no way tantamount to a criminal conviction. It merely expresses the Senators' doubts about the appointee's fitness. Such doubts should be resolved *against* the nominee and *for* the public interest. Throughout the second Bush's presidency, reactionary defenders of the imperial presidency challenged the U.S. Constitution itself. According to these defenders, the Senate's role in approving presidential nominees is not, as specified in the Constitution, to *advise and consent*, but merely to *consent*.

The NRA strikes again

Another mindboggling reversal of proof burden was embodied in the legal criteria for judging restoration of gun-owning rights to psychologically sick persons previously judged incompetent to bear arms. Following the 2007 Virginia Tech massacre by a deranged murderer, whose 33 victims constituted the worst mass shooting in American history, Congress defied the NRA by passing a law designed to make it more difficult for the mentally ill to get guns. Through its always formidable power of political intimidation, the NRA successfully demanded provisions for restoring gun rights for the mentally ill. In California, a fairly rigorous procedure for restoring gun rights was jeopardized by an incomprehensible burden-of-proof requirement. Under the California statute, the district attorney bears the burden of proof to demonstrate that the petitioner ". . . would not be likely to use firearms in a safe and lawful manner."

What the statute's authors overlooked was the obvious illogic in reversing the burden of proof in these cases. In the original termination of gun-owning rights, the state obviously bears the burden of proof. Otherwise gun rights could be arbitrarily revoked. But once the mentally ill person has been expertly diagnosed and legally classified, the burden of proof is logically reversed. The petitioner should then bear the burden of proving his fitness for gun ownership. Placing the burden of proof on the district attorney to demonstrate that the mentally ill person would not be a safe risk with guns contains an absurd logical implication: i.e., that the original, legally validated diagnosis of mental illness was an error. That implication would require continual diagnoses, proving and continually reproving the person's mental incapacity. As the only reasonable resolution, the petitioner obviously should be required to prove his fitness to own a gun.

Even Guiltier

Like the previous discussion of Senator Fulbright's exposure of the Vietnam War as an exercise in burden-of-proof reversal, the Iraq War exhibited the same logical failure. If there is ever a time to hold advocates guilty until proven innocent, it is against those who would launch a war on the basis of unsubstantiated evidence. Against the Bush administration's case for the Iraq War, there was superabundant, heavily documented evidence that its neoconservative masterminds used 9/11 as an excuse to launch a war they had wanted for years.

President Bush's preposterous May, 2003, "Mission-Accomplished" speech aboard the Abe Lincoln aircraft carrier was a compendium of megalomaniacal lies and fantasy, the product of a second-rate mind that believed it communicated with God. In his deludedly optimistic declaration of victory, Bush betrayed his hopeless delusion: "In these 19 months that changed the world (i.e., the time between 9/11 and "mission-accomplished" day), our actions have been focused and deliberate and proportionate to the offense. We have not forgotten the victims of September the 11th, the last phone calls, the cold murder of children, the searches in the rubble. With those attacks, the terrorists and their supporters declared war on the United States, and war is what they got."

Earlier in the speech, Bush had unequivocally linked Saddam Hussein and Iraq to the 9/11 attacks. "That terrible morning, 19 evil men, the shock troops of a hateful ideology, gave America and the civilized world a glimpse of their ambition. They imagined, in the words of one terrorist, that September the 11ᵗʰ would be the beginning of the end for America."

What Bush omitted, of course, was that nearly 80 percent of the 19 terrorists were Saudis, and that none were Iraqis. For the small minority of Americans who know the basic facts, Bush's hopeless delusions were obvious. It was unnecessary to know the later documented revelations about Bush's and Cheney's deceptive plotting to justify the war.

And that, of course, is the most vital lesson to be learned from this disastrous military adventure. In any undertaking as important as war, and even in most political enterprises of less importance, proponents should bear the burden of proof. The Pentagon's weapons-development projects — notably, President *Reagan's fantastic "Star Wars" project, after a third of a century of perennial failure -- exists only because of defective, reversed burden-of-proof logic.* Like the Iraq War, Star Wars survives because the burden of proof has always been on skeptics rather than proponents. They invariably have gigantic conflicts of interest against giving honest opinions, which would endanger a project whose continuance means millions to their defense-contractor employers.

In projects like Star Wars, as in actual wars, the criterion should be:

Guilty until proven innocent.

CHAPTER 4

Sliding Down the Slippery Slope

"There are more fools than knaves in the world, else the knaves wouldn't have enough to live on."

Samuel Butler

A popular, all-purpose argument for opposing reforms of any variety, the slippery-slope fallacy relies on a simple-minded metaphor. Any action to improve any government program, or to alleviate a social, economic, or political evil, must inevitably initiate a disastrous series of events ending in catastrophe. No brakes can stop these disastrous events once they get started. They build unstoppable momentum as the reform program, dislodged from its safely anchored position in the level plateau of the status quo, careens down the icy slope into the horrors of the valley below.

Slippery justices

In this era of hyper-irrationality, use of the slippery-slope fallacy has naturally proliferated. According to a linguist who can speak with authority, the "slippery-slope" phrase has multiplied seven times in two decades. In its most alarming recent manifestation the slippery-slope fallacy has appeared in Supreme Court arguments. Debating the health-care reform legislation case, two "conservative" justices cited the slippery slope as grounds for their votes against the reform legislation. Here's Justice Antonin Scalia's ludicrous slippery-slope argument. "Everybody has to buy food. . . . So you define a market as food. Therefore everybody is in the market. Therefore you make people buy broccoli."

It is difficult to believe that Justice Scalia's argument was serious. It was an excuse, not a reason, for his predictable negative vote against health-care reform. Owing to a surprise reversal of Justice Roberts's normal conservative sympathies, the reactionary justices failed in their efforts to kill the Obama health-care reform.

The slippery-slope fallacy played a big role in one of the Supreme Court's worst decisions. In the justice-denying decision, *District Attorney v. Osborne*, the Supreme Court's politically reactionary majority rejected a prisoner's request for DNA testing that could prove his innocence after 14 years' imprisonment on a probably false rape verdict. In the most appalling aspect of this decision, Chief Justice John Roberts agreed with Alaskan prosecutors that a DNA test could definitively determine the prisoner's guilt or innocence. In his ruling opinion, however, he saw "no necessity for a far-reaching constitutional right of access to this type of evidence." (In other words, don't confuse the courts with scientific facts.)

In a concurring opinion, Justice Sam Alito buttressed Roberts's opinion with a slippery-slope warning. DNA testing could induce prisoners "to play games with the criminal justice system," said Justice Alito. They could drown state courts in a flood of testing demands, argued Alito, in typical exploitation of the slippery-slope fallacy.

Alito's charge contradicts the facts. Cardoza University's DNA-based Project Innocence has won 240 exonerations of falsely convicted prisoners, concurrently identifying 103 guilty, unconvicted perpetrators identified for corrective prosecution. Project Innocence achieved these corrective results despite its acceptance of only 1 percent of its applications. There was no slippery slope, no avalanche of demands for DNA testing.

The horrors of gun control

As the leading lobbyist for its industry, the National Rifle Association (NRA) opposes effective gun control with the slippery-slope fallacy, and its paranoid adherents swallow this nonsense with gargantuan gullibility. Ever since his 2008 election, President Obama has been called a dedicated opponent of the Second Amendment by NRA executive vice president Wayne LaPierre. The slightest tightening of our incredibly lax gun laws — banning gun sales to persons on the terrorist watch list, or extending background checks to buyers at gun shows — is denounced as the first step on a sinister plan to confiscate all guns. On two notable occasions, Obama's 2008 and 2012 election victories, this absurd argument has inspired thousands of gullible dupes to rush out to buy guns before it is too late. This, against a President whose only gun-related laws concerned two votes, one of which extended gun-bearing rights to national parks.

A clever letter-to-the-editor *New York Times* reader turned the slippery-slope fallacy around. If a ban on 30-round magazine clips would inevitably lead to a total ban, why wouldn't any relaxation of gun laws lead to 100-round magazines, stockpiles of grenades, shoulder-launched missiles, flame throwers, even citizen-owned thermonuclear bombs? Even the NRA's most rabid followers accept some constitutional limits. But they never see the slippery-slope in reverse. Yet a progressive increase in legal weapons is logically no more improbable than a total ban.

Slippery lobbyists

A congressional bill to repeal a 75-year-old law banning the jamming of telecommunication messages offers a classic illustration of slippery-slope logic. Here's the problem requiring remedial legislative action: cellphones smuggled into prisons enable prisoners to plot crimes. In Baltimore, for a horrible example, convict Patrick Byers used a smuggled cellphone to order the assassination of a witness who testified against him. (A federal jury gave Byers a life sentence for plotting this murder.) Other crimes resulting from smuggled cellphones include extortion, tax evasion, drug deals, credit-card fraud, riot plotting, and prison escapes.

But the obvious answer of jamming convicted criminals' phones is rejected by cell-phone industry lobbyists. Why? Because allowing the jamming of criminals' phones will inevitably lead to the jamming of any phone for any reason. We must thus accept the status quo, regardless of its evils, because any remedy would be worse, a dismal outcome guaranteed by the slippery-slope argument.

The end of free speech?

Hate-crime laws, augmenting punishments for murder and other crimes incited by racial, religious, or anti-gay prejudice, naturally attract slippery-slope rebuttals. Evangelical Christians argued that a proposed federal hate-crime law was a potential infringement of First-Amendment free-speech guarantees. Suppose a clergyman preached against homosexuality by quoting Leviticus 20:13:

> *"If a man lie with mankind, as he lieth with a woman, both of them have committed an abomination: they shall surely be put to death; their blood shall be upon them."*

This idiotic fear prompted the bill's sponsor, Senator Pat Leahy (D, VT) to include a provision explicitly assuring First-Amendment protection to anyone expressing moral objections to homosexuality. It was, of course, needless. But it was a small price to pay for at least partial alleviation of the imaginary problem.

That it was needless is easily demonstrated. For decades anti-abortionists have preached hatred of abortion doctors, condemned for murdering thousands of children by demagogues like Fox News's Bill O'Reilly. Yet no one has ever been indicted for incitement to murder. The First Amendment protects this odious hate speech, and it will predictably continue to do so. Fears that hate-crime laws pose a threat to free speech are proven preposterous by the free-speech exercise of anti-abortionists who continually refer to abortion doctors as baby killers. The anti-hate crimers are made ridiculous by their past exercise of the most extreme free speech without the slightest threat of prosecution.

Averted horrors

Oregon's pioneering Death-with-Dignity Act, finally implemented in 1997 after a three-year delay attributable chiefly to Catholic Church opposition, provides a thunderous refutation of the slippery-slope fallacy. The state's physician-assisted-suicide (PAS) law, allows a "capable" adult with life expectancy of six months or less to request a lethal drug dose. Two physicians must certify the request; either physician may order the patient's psychological evaluation; and the patient must administer the lethal drug.

Opponents depicted a cascade of slippery-slope horrors following approval of PAS. Hitler's euthanasia program lay with inexorable certainty at the bottom of the slope. From the right of suffering terminal patients to relief from their pain, the Death with Dignity Act would inevitably metasticize into a morally cancerous program to kill the elderly, the infirm, and the poor.

Nothing remotely resembling these horrors has occurred since PAS was enacted. An annual average of 25 Oregonians have availed themselves of its beneficence. They were predominantly white, well educated, and adequately insured. They merely demanded the right to make this ultimate life-or-death decision, free of interference by doctors or religious zealots attempting to force their private morality ("Only God has the right to determine your exact time of death") on those who reject the busybodies' moral dictatorship.

Despite the 18-year experience with Oregon's PAS statute, only one other state, neighboring Washington, in 2008, has enacted similar legislation. National polls show overwhelming popular support for PAS. But the obstructive minority, energized by its zealous adherents, can easily intimidate anxious state legislators into persistent non-action. Regardless of a political issue's merits, they almost always buckle under attack by a willful minority. Fear is a more potent political weapon than hope. In the slippery-slope fallacy, obstructionists have an ideal argument: to bear those evils we know rather than fly to those we know not of. In some instances, of course, our natural conservatism doubtless shields us from ill-designed, harmful actions. But the slippery-slope fallacy tilts this conservative proclivity far out of beneficent balance.

Of dominos and slopes

The widely publicized domino theory, the rationalization upon which the Vietnam War's justification was founded, relied on slippery-slope reasoning. It was formulated long before the United States became militarily involved in Vietnam. A full decade before United States troops entered that conflict, in an April, 1954, press conference, President Dwight Eisenhower stated the domino theory:

"If someone sets up a row of dominos, and knocks over the first one ... it is certain that the last one will go over very quickly. It would be the beginning of a disintegration that would have the most profound influences ..." The loss of Indo-China (i.e., Vietnam) would lead to the loss of Burma, Thailand, Malay peninsula, and Indonesia.

For two decades, the domino theory was cited as the reason to continue this hopeless conflict. Lost in the persistent recriminations about Vietnam is the colossal error at the core of this geopolitical hypothesis. According to the domino theory, an American loss in Vietnam would assure that other Asian nations would topple like dominos into the Soviet orbit, as President Eisenhower predicted in 1954. But contrary to that fatally flawed thesis, despite our loss in Vietnam, we *won* the Cold War. Vietnam, it turned out, was merely a local, nationalistic war, with no significant connection to the great power struggle between the United States and the Soviet Union. Vietnam levied tremendous costs: 58,000 American lives and several hundred billion dollars wasted in this futile venture. But judged from a geopolitical viewpoint, our Vietnam loss was harmless.

American neoconservatives flaunt their tribal values in their continuing recriminations about Vietnam, 40 years after the war's end. The United States could have won, say these diehards, if the lying liberal press hadn't undermined the war effort with its negative reporting. This tribalist delusion requires plenty of lies to sustain it. Contrary to conservative mythology, the Vietnam War entailed our intervention in a civil war. Vietnam was one nation, divided into two segments by a treaty-negotiated demarcation line as a temporary boundary until the country could be reunited through an internationally supervised election. When Secretary of State John Foster Dulles foresaw electoral defeat for the American-sponsored South, he canceled the election.

Conservatives lament Vietnam as a loss of national prestige, prompting the world to hold the United States in contempt, a paper Tiger unwilling to sacrifice for victory. Yet the very men who maintain this hypothesis — conservatives like former Vice President Dick Cheney, former Deputy Defense Secretary Paul Wolfowitz, journalist Bill Kristol, Rush Limbaugh, and many others — are the very ones who hastened defeat in this unwinnable war through their cowardly draft dodging. What ended the war was less recognition of its futility (though that was a factor) than the refusal of lower-class youths to bear the total burden of fighting it. When the sons of the rich were forced to take their chances with the military draft, support for the war collapsed.

Neoconservative logic is as phony as its superpatriotism. Conservatives' refusal to recognize the fallacy of the domino theory parallels their hypocrisy in posing as superpatriots willing to sacrifice others' lives for their causes in Iraq as well as Vietnam.

Grandma's got to go

President Obama's health-reform legislation inevitably evoked slippery-slope logic from Republican opponents. They seized on a trivial provision that would allow physician reimbursement for end-of-life counseling. For anyone concerned about Medicare's excessive cost, the huge expenditures on largely useless efforts to prolong blighted lives through ventilators, intravenous feeding, and useless resuscitation obviously require limitation. Medicare expenses incurred in the last year of life account for a quarter of the program's cost. It's an absurd imbalance, diverting medical resources from more productive use on younger patients whose treatment would yield greater benefits than prolonging lives of comatose, or otherwise incapacitated patients for a few weeks or months.

To House Minority Leader John Boehner, however, the mere idea of voluntary end-of-life counseling puts us on a terrifying slippery slope. "This provision may start us down a treacherous path toward government-encouraged euthanasia," warned Rep. Boehner. Boehner's warning was a model of restraint compared with other Republican changes. For Sarah Palin, the slippery slope is much too tame a metaphor. Instead of a slide down the icy trail, Mrs. Palin sees a record ski jump of 800 meters, plunging us immediately into Rep. Boehner's future horrors. Here's what Mrs. Palin said:

> *"The America I know and love is not*
> *the one in which my parents or my baby*
> *with Down Syndrome will have to*
> *stand in front of Obama's death panel*
> *so his bureaucrats can decide, based on*

a subjective judgment of their 'level of
productivity in society' whether they are
worthy of health care."

The next step is obvious: extermination camps patterned on Belsen and Buchenwald.

The slippery-slope fallacy leads inexorably to cruder weapons exploited in the special-interest war against health-care reform. Wealthy interest groups helped to organize mobs, encouraged by Sean Hannity and Rush Limbaugh, to disrupt town-hall meetings. They shouted down Congressmen's efforts to explain the bill's provisions. Prominent among the opponents of reform is Conservatives for Patients' Rights (CPR). This organization is run by Rick Scott, forced out of his job as chief executive officer of a hospital chain, Columbia HRA, that was fined $1.7 billion –– yes, $1.7 billion –– for overbilling state and federal health plans.

The protesting mobs displayed an incredible degree of ignorance. At a Texas congressman's town-hall meeting, an activist opponent of reform asked attendees if they opposed ". . . socialized or government-run health care." Nearly all raised their hands. Then Rep. Gene Green asked how many were on Medicare. Nearly half raised their hands. They evidently didn't know that Medicare was a government-run health-care plan. In a Mississippi meeting attendees heard a rabid constituent parroting the talk-show charge that Obama's plan was "Marxist." In Tennessee police were called in when furious protesters got unruly. In Missouri a town-hall meeting was cancelled to avoid a riot.

In this and other contexts the slippery-slope is merely the first step in a campaign to suppress rational debate. It's the ideal means for evoking primitive fear. It is perpetrated by people who maintain piously controlled straight faces as they accuse political opponents of attempting to suppress free speech.

CHAPTER 5

The Single-Entry
Bookkeeping Fallacy

"The man who holds that every human right is secondary to his profit must now give way to the advocate of human welfare, who rightly maintains that every man holds his property subject to the general right of the community to regulate its use to whatever degree the public welfare may require it."

Theodore Roosevelt
1910

Coined by David Stockman when he was President Reagan's young budget director in the early 1980s, the phrase "single-entry bookkeeping" refers to political ideologues' proclivity for counting only the negative aspects of projects they oppose and the positive aspects of projects they support. Since the invention of double-entry bookkeeping during the late Renaissance, business accounting has required the listing of liabilities as well as assets as a means of impartially reporting a business enterprise's financial status, on an appropriately named balance sheet. As demonstrated by the recent financial meltdown, resulting from recklessly corrupt and prime mortgage lending, "creative accounting" still allows dishonest business reporting. But the double-entry format makes it more difficult to dupe investors and others concerned with financial affairs.

For an egregious illustration of single-entry bookkeeping, consider conservative economist Martin Feldstein's argument against President Obama's jobs-creation act. Feldstein disparaged the President's plan for its excessive cost per created job. He estimated this cost at $200,000 per job, a figure obtained by dividing the total cost of $450 million by 2 million created jobs. Feldstein's calculation counts the liabilities — i.e., the $450-million cost — but almost totally ignores the assets. According to Feldstein, the $140 billion proposed for infrastructure maintenance and repair of highways, bridges, and school repair, and the billions proposed for hiring of more teachers produces essentially nothing of value. Carried to its logical conclusion, we would never spend public money on anything if it produces no assets. The American Society of Civil Engineers (ASCE) has estimated a backlog of some $2 trillion to rebuild our deteriorated infrastructure. And it's not only bridges and highways. Our leaking sewer lines, many more than a half century old, are polluting our water supply, and these water lines, too, are deteriorating from age. When their rupture floods highways, they waste millions of man-hours lost in needless traffic jams. Our dams are similarly disintegrating, plagued by decades of neglect. Conservatives count private expenditures for gambling casinos, alcohol consumption, and Nascar races for more than education, efficient transportation, clean air and water.

Leave it to former House Speaker Newt Gingrich to top Feldstein's version of single-entry bookkeeping. Gingrich claimed that the alleged five jobs created by a solar-energy subsidy cost taxpayers $10 million per job. This is single-entry bookkeeping with a fiendish vengeance. The $50-million solar-energy subsidy would provide solar power for 17,000 homes. Gingrich considers that asset totally worthless.

In the political world, benefit/cost analysis is the counterpart of double-entry bookkeeping in the financial world. Ideally, any legislative bill or other proposed political action is judged by an objective listing of benefits and costs. Only if the benefits exceed the costs should the legislation be enacted. But, of course, politicians promoting their favorite causes seldom pay any attention to costs. They focus solely on benefits. Farm subsidies and mortgage subsidies — notably, the mortgage-interest tax deduction, which costs the government some $130 billion annually — illustrate the benefits-only approach. Proponents of mortgage-interest tax deductions never admit the tremendous fiscal problems and the disproportionate benefit to wealthy mortgagors attributable to this tax deduction. Proponents count only the presumed benefit of government subsidization of home ownership.

Unplanned parenthood

To some degree, single-entry bookkeeping characterizes both major political parties. Social conservatives, however, are the chief offenders. Perhaps the worst example is the anti-abortionists' adamant refusal to consider the evil consequences of their cause. An old Jules Feiffer cartoon corrects the view of extremist symmetry. Commenting on the 1954 school-desegregation decision, *Brown v. Board of Education*, President Eisenhower is depicted as saying, "I'm against the extremists on both sides: those who want to close the schools and those who want to keep them open." Emotionally moderate people are vulnerable to the absurdity illustrated by Eisenhower's statement. They tend to believe that passionate conviction on either side of a controversy indicates extremism.

The general failure to understand anti-abortion fanaticism is evident in Roger Rosenblatt's *New York Times Magazine* article, "How To End the Abortion War," published some 15 years ago. Rosenblatt indicated no comprehension of the basic issue between anti-abortionists and pro-choice advocates. That issue is between (a) those who believe in the right to privacy promulgated by the 1973 Supreme Court in its *Roe v. Wade* decision, and (b) those who believe that the government should force unwilling women to bear unwanted babies. As a compromise, Rosenblatt proposed an abortion-legalizing law accompanied by sex education, designed to promote birth control as a means of reducing the need for abortion. But most anti-abortionists oppose birth control as virulently as they oppose abortion. Rosenblatt's proffered compromise has always been accepted by pro-choice proponents and rejected by anti-abortionists.

Knowing that opposition to birth control is a much less popular cause than anti-abortionism, anti-abortionists generally remain silent about their anti-contraception sentiments. An exception to this general rule, but nonetheless representative of the anti-abortionist position, is Judy Brown, president of the American Life League. Ms. Brown, a prominent philosopher of this reactionary revival of the sex-policing morality of the Middle Ages, explains her organization's expanding goal. "We see a direct connection between the practice of contraception and the practice of abortion. The mindset that invites a couple to use contraception is an anti-child mindset. So when a baby is conceived accidentally, the couple already have (sic) this negative attitude toward the child. Therefore seeking an abortion is a natural outcome. *We oppose all forms of contraception.*" (emphasis added).

Though he never made a candid public declaration on this subject, President George W. Bush obviously agreed with Ms. Brown. His 2002 appointee to the Food and Drug Administration (FDA's) Reproductive Health Drugs Advising Committee, Dr. Joseph B. Stanford, shares Ms. Brown's sentiments. "Sexual union and marriage ought to be a complete giving of each spouse to the other, and when fertility is deliberately excluded from giving, I am convinced that something is lost. A husband will . . . begin to see his wife as an object of pleasure who should always be available for gratification," said Dr. Stanford.

Anti-abortionists' refusal to consider the consequences of their cause indicates a transcendent moral fervor that renders all practical consequences beyond discussion. The roughly 2 million abortions annually performed in the United States are concentrated in lower-class blacks, whose illegitimacy rate would otherwise be much higher than its current socially catastrophic 70 percent. It has been redundantly demonstrated that unwanted babies born to poor, uneducated minorities are doomed at birth to a host of evils. They are 17 times as likely to grow up as criminals as kids born to affluent families. They face similarly bleak odds against being employed, against averting welfare, plus a higher probability of suffering a host of mental and social problems. Economists have traced the decline of criminal statistics beginning in the early 1990s to the reduction of unwanted babies aborted after the 1973 *Roe v. Wade* Supreme Court decision.

Moral fervor v. common sense

Anti-abortionists are nonetheless contemptuous of these practical arguments against forcing women to bear unwanted children This contempt is so great that they generally refuse even to refute them. Moral fervor elevates them above the banal necessity of considering how their cause would, and does insofar as its harassing tactics are successful, increase the sum total of human misery. Note, too, that as political ultraconservatives, they accept no responsibility for alleviating this misery. It was no exaggeration to say of Ronald Reagan's presidency, which instituted the Republican Party's fanatical anti-abortion policy (with no exemptions for rape and incest), that Reagan believed the government's responsibility began with conception and ended at birth. (It's also interesting to note that Reagan's zealous anti-abortionism originated roughly a decade after he signed the nation's most liberal abortion-permitting law as California's governor.)

There is no better example of single-entry bookkeeping than the anti-abortion movement.

The anti-abortionists' one minor concession to consideration of liabilities concerns the pretense that adoption of unwanted babies is a viable alternative to abortion. But even with the relief provided by several hundred thousand annually aborted black fetuses, black babies are still a huge drug on the adoption market. If the supply of these unwanted babies was magnified by the outlawing of all abortions, the adoption alternative would be even less — far less — practicable than its currently dismal status.

Buttressing their use of the single-entry bookkeeping fallacy, anti-abortionists exploit other perversions of logic discussed elsewhere in this book. References to the murder of "unborn children" reminds me of uncomposed symphonies and unwritten novels. And to consider a fertilized egg a full-fledged human being, as proposed by lawmakers in several states, is logically equivalent to calling an acorn an oak tree.

Like Christian evangelicals on other issues, the anti-abortionists' claim to high morality is betrayed by their perennial resort to lies, deceit, and general intellectual dishonesty. In an article entitled "Right to Lie," *Scientific American* corrected the anti-abortionist lie that abortion is more dangerous than childbirth. (It's actually safer.) Anti-abortionists have also falsely claimed that abortion increases breast-cancer risk. Anxious female respondents to an advertised toll-free telephone number were told that an abortion would raise their breast-cancer risk to 50 percent probability. That's another gigantic lie.

Former U.S. Senator (and failed 2012 Republican presidential candidate) Rick Santorum also stretches his anti-abortion argument far beyond the single-entry bookkeeping fallacy. Here's Santorum's incredible statement: "To put rape or incest victims through the trauma of abortion, I think is too much to ask." It is, of course, Santorum and his fellow anti-abortionist fanatics who want the government to force rape victims not in into the imaginary trauma of freely chosen abortion, but into the real trauma of government-enforced birth of their rapists' babies.

Welfare promotion

Liberal ideologues come close to matching ultraconservative anti-abortionists in their dedication to single-entry bookkeeping. United States welfare policy in the 1960s and 1970s was apparently designed to perpetuate minority dependence on the federal government. (Rush Limbaugh bases his career on an endless, exaggerated repetition of this thesis as being the Democrats' all-pervasive ultimate goal.) Before President Bill Clinton signed a mid-1990s' bill, allegedly ending welfare as we know it, federal policy rewarded welfare recipients for having additional children with absolutely no consideration whether they could afford them. Breeding in heedless promiscuity, welfare mothers gained additional federal payments for having additional children. The so-called Aid-to-Dependent-Children program encouraged out-of-wedlock births through the policy of subsidizing them without limit. It also allowed teenage mothers to apply for their own government-finfanced apartments.

Conservatives rightly condemned this policy for what it obviously was: financial encouragement for reckless, irresponsible sexual behavior, especially by males accepting no responsibility for bearing the costs of their breeding habits. In the ghetto philosophy, unfortunately, these irresponsible impregnators reigned as cultural heroes, fulfilling the primitive pride in procreation without incurring any of its responsibilities. Even if they saw anything wrong in this attitude, liberal ideologues generally excused it as an inevitable concomitant of racist prejudice.

Liberal ideologues denounced any effort to remove the perverse incentive to irresponsible breeding as an attack on ghetto dwellers. Like the anti-abortionists' refusal to consider the social consequences of their policy, liberal ideologues refused to confront the problem of 32-year-old grandmothers in Newark, New Jersey, and other central cities.

The late Senator Daniel Patrick Moynihan had warned about the black family's disintegration back in 1965, when he published data showing a 70 percent out-of-wedlock black birth rate. White liberal ideologues and black leaders accused Moynihan of racism for publicizing these harsh truths, though no one challenged their validity. When black leaders like entertainer Bill Cosby warned the black community about this problem, they were denounced for lack of compassion. According to a prominent black Washington Post columnist, it was not the government's business to tell black welfare recipients how many babies to bear. Moynihan's advice "to make the daddies pay" was generally ignored. Despite its demonstrable success, New Jersey's efforts to reduce welfare mothers' birth rates, by cutting off aid at two children, were denounced as simultaneously ineffective and immoral. And so, for widely disparate reasons, anti-abortionists and their liberal opponents are united in opposition to effective action against illegitimate black births with their devastating consequences for the victims' prospects for decent productive lives. Both practice single-entry bookkeeping, refusing to count the costs of their advocated policies.

Single-entry bookkeeping, oppositional style

Single-entry bookkeeping flourishes not only in ignoring deleterious consequences, but in creating imaginary deleterious consequences — i.e., by ignoring the benefits while exaggerating the liabilities of proposed policies. After the catastrophic financial meltdown produced by the Bush Administration's deregulatory fervor, creation of the Consumer Financial Protection Bureau (CFPB) was a no-brainer. President Obama's choice to head this agency, Elizabeth Warren, was the ideal nominee. She articulated her goals with pellucid clarity — to require credit-card and mortgage contracts without the confusing, longwinded legalese, invariably printed in microscopic type, and obviously designed to mislead consumers about exorbitant penalties and interest rates. With typical timidity, refusing to wage a principled battle against Republican obstructionists obsessed with his political destruction, President Obama failed to nominate Warren as the CFPB director.

To the bankers' lobby, Mrs. Warren was the counterpart of a financial Hitler, determined to perpetrate a political Holocaust against bankers. Brief, clear contracts pose a threat to the capitalist system, say the bankers. Among the ultimate horrors of requiring honestly worded contracts, warning consumers of the precise conditions under which they are subject to exorbitant penalty payments and interest rates, is the threat to "financial innovation." The most remarkable thing about this claim is the banking lobby's ability to maintain serious expressions while making it. If what the bankers claim is true, there could be no better argument for the CFPB than its presumed threat to "financial innovation." Financial innovation is what caused the financial meltdown following the subprime mortgage fiasco. If financial innovation had not created collectivised debt obligations (CDOs) comprising millions of home mortgages, the subprime mortgage fiasco not only *would* not have occurred; it *could* not have occurred.

CDOs became popular with the financial community for obvious reasons. By bundling mortgages into large unit packages, bankers could provide pension funds and other large investors with ostensibly safe investment opportunities. For the mortgage bankers, the benefits were twofold. By selling their individual mortgages to purveyors of CDOs, mortgage bankers freed up capital immobilized by its individual loan status. They could then originate as many as 10 times their original mortgage investments. Even worse for financial securities, once they unloaded their mortgages into CDOs purchased by others, they were no longer responsible for the security of the individual mortgages. By passing that responsibility onto CDO investors, the original mortgage lender's motivation underwent a thorough transmogrification. His prime concern now became how to maximize his profits. This obviously entailed increasing the number of originated mortgages, not the safety of the investment. Under these drastically altered conditions, lending standards naturally collapsed Crooked mortgage lenders like the notorious Countrywide required their personnel to approve loans for anyone with a pulse. (According to Countryside employees, they were instructed *never* to turn down any applicant, regardless of risk.) In extreme instances, mortgagors with $15,000 incomes were issued $700,000 mortgages. Applicants were encouraged to lie about their incomes. Lured by the promise of free-lunch profits, bankers jumped on the bandwagon.

The ultimate collapse was inevitable. Reckless speculation paid off for years. The complex bundling of individual securities and then of bundles of bundles created global financial tangles almost impossible to unravel. The biggest banks often charged mortgagors with fraudulently exaggerated debts. They sometimes forced foreclosures on homeowners who had no mortgages. Their documentation often violated the law. It was so slovenly that the courts have rejected thousands of foreclosure proceedings. Credit-rating agencies classified bonds subsequently reduced to junk status as gilt-edged AAA securities. And in another innovation, so-called credit default swaps permitted Goldman Sachs and other financial giants to gamble on insurance contracts. This practice was analogous to allowing an outsider to buy fire insurance on a third-party's house, with the consequent motive to commit arson.

All this financial finagling was justified as an immense boon to the overall economy. Meanwhile it magnified the financial industry's profits to an incredible 40 percent of *all* corporate profits from 16 percent in 1980.

The list of evils perpetuated by the single-entry bookkeeping fallacy could be expanded indefinitely. The American Civil Liberties Union (ACLU) has mounted many worthwhile projects defending constitutional freedoms. But it also champions trivial causes that emphasize personal freedom without corresponding responsibility. Some years ago, when restaurant owners installed washroom surveillance cameras to assure that food-handling employees were washing their hands, a vital safeguard against food poisoning, the ACLU countered with this condemnation: "Every American has an expectation that when they (sic) go to the bathroom what they do is their own private business." Patrons sickened by a restaurant employee's failure to wash his hands might disagree.

Single-entry bookkeeping has perpetuated the useless, costly War on Drugs, whose proponents obdurately refuse to consider its gargantuan liabilities. In its 40-plus futile years of existence, it has cost roughly $1 trillion, with no discernible benefits.

In the first U.S. experiment with this kind of morally based legislation, the prohibition of alcohol lasted a mere 13 years. Its chief accomplishment was the establishment of organized crime as a national institution. The equally futile War on Drugs has itself become an institution, defended fiercely by prison guards and others with a vested interest in perpetuating this folly. Social conservatives, the vast majority of whom are also anti-abortionists, view the War on Drugs as a transcendent moral issue. It also displays the hypocrisy of those who denounce regulation in the abstract, but support it in practice.

Occasional newspaper editorials cite the drug war's most obviously harmful consequence -- i.e., the persistent, escalating drug-inspired Mexican mass murders, which are driving that benighted nation to the brink of degenerating into a failed state, unable to perform its role of providing domestic security. Mexico's drug violence obviously springs from our War on Drugs. Without American criminalization of narcotics, the estimated $30-billion-plus annual cost of Mexico's drugs would drastically shrink, thus removing the huge profits that keep Mexico's drug gangs in business. American-exported firearms constitute some 90 percent of the Mexican drug gangs' firepower. To our dedicated drug warriors and the virtually omnipotent NRA, Mexico's drug violence is of no concern. Zealots of the drug war and the NRA are among the most dedicated practitioners of single-entry bookkeeping.

Among other logical fallacies, George W. Bush's decision to plunge into the Iraq War provides another devastating illustration of the single-entry bookkeeping fallacy. By some administration officials, the war's liabilities were counted as assets. Deputy Defense Secretary Paul Wolfowitz's claim that Iraq's oil would finance the war is an extreme example. The Iraq War, of course, exemplifies several logical fallacies -- notably, the previously discussed burden-of-proof reversal. Logical fallacies often congregate in multi-faceted combinations, beginning with distortions of fact and then followed by slovenly logic. Single-entry bookkeeping is one of the most pervasive of these fallacies.

CHAPTER 6

Herrings (Red) and Straw Men

"It is just as important that business keep out of government as that government keep out of business."

Herbert Hoover
1928

Among the major weapons in the reactionary ideologues' forensic arsenal, the red herring fallacy is a strong contender for first place. Derived from the practice of using dried-smoked (i.e., "red") herrings to train scent-sniffing hounds, the "red herring" refers to a "misleading clue or distraction," according to my dictionary. Through bountiful use of red herrings, ideologues can effect total changes of embarrassing subjects and dupe their simple-minded votaries into righteously indignant crusades against imaginary evils.

Learning from lawyers

Those traditional masters of deception, the lawyers, have long served as forensic models for politicians. In O.J. Simpson's 1995 criminal trial, the defense team staged perhaps the boldest, most successful ever use of the red-herring fallacy, to free a vicious killer. Starting with Simpson defender Johnny Cochran's opening diatribe, the defense team's red-herring strategy was painfully obvious. Cochran and his colleagues depicted the Los Angeles Police Department (LAPD) as a racist organization determined to convict its celebrity black client at all costs. In what Simpson's lawyers called "a rush to judgment, the Los Angeles had refused to target "the real killers." Instead, they tried to convict a defendant they allegedly knew to be innocent.

Simpson's lawyers desperately needed this racist red herring to divert jurors' attention from a devastating agglomeration of technically solid circumstantial evidence. Ubiquitous blood DNA from Simpson and his two victims proved beyond a shadow of a doubt that Simpson was guilty. Dr. Edward Blake, probably the nation's foremost expert on DNA forensics, was retained to coach Simpson lawyers Barry Scheck and Peter Neufeld in their devious attacks on hapless LAPD criminologists. After Simpson's acquittal, when his statements had no effect on the verdict, Dr. Blake made this startling admission: the DNA evidence proving Simpson's guilt was "unassailable."

As further proof that they knew Simpson was guilty, his lawyers rejected prosecutor Marcia Clark's offer to provide them with DNA evidence so they could conduct their own tests. That prospect, however, would have demolished the defense strategy, which attacked DNA evidence as planted, contaminated, and generally falsified. The defense couldn't risk additional test results proving Simpson's guilt.

By a lucky coincidence for the defense, one key LAPD policeman, the notorious Detective Mark Fuhrmann, became the defense team's scapegoat, making the prosecution's case hopeless. At Simpson's Rockingham estate, Detective Fuhrmann had discovered the blood-stained glove worn by Simpson when he committed the murders. He was also caught committing gratuitous perjury. Audio tapes record his boast about planting false evidence against black defendants in North Carolina. In these tapes, Fuhrmann was recorded using the N word countless times, contradicting his previous testimony that he had never done so. Confronted with proof of his perjury, Fuhrmann serially pleaded the Fifth Amendment's protection against self-incrimination. Fuhrmann's disgraceful performance demolished whatever faint hope had previously existed for Simpson's conviction. His racism was a perfect red herring for convincing the uneducated jurors that Simpson was innocent.

Logically Fuhrmann's racism was totally irrelevant. The DNA evidence was incontrovertible, as the defense team's DNA expert admitted in a post-trial interview. Displaying the legal system's obsession with prejudice, Judge Lance Ito had barred regular newspaper readers from jury duty. This, of course, assured a low juror educational level, people incapable of following the prosecution's expert testimony about DNA biochemistry and the accompanying statistical inferences. As one commentator summed up the irony of the Simpson trial, "For decades, good 'ol boy lawyers had been pulling off the same stunt in courtrooms all across Dixie, winning unfathomable verdicts from redneck juries for defendants accused of murdering African Americans. All Cochran did was switch the scenario."

Revenge against Rather

Red herrings work just as well in the political arena as in the courts. The controversy culminating in the 2005 firing of veteran CBS evening news anchor Dan Rather provides another classic illustration of the red-herring fallacy. It was skillfully augmented by the "kill-the-messenger" psychology dating from antiquity.

As background for this case, the 2004 presidential campaign featured Karl Rove's characteristic strategy of turning the opposing candidate's strength against him. Thrice-decorated

Vietnam veteran John Kerry was attacked by a scurrilous gang of Republican veterans as unpatriotic, whereas the draft-dodging President, George W. Bush, was presented as a maliciously vilified paragon of patriotism. This Looking-Glass logic had worked for the Republicans in the 2002 Georgia senatorial race between incumbent triple-amputee, Vietnam veteran Max Cleland vs. Vietnam draft-dodger Saxbe Chambliss. To the Republican party, a draft-dodging Republican is almost always more patriotic than a decorated Democratic military hero. Especially in the rebel Southern states, with their Civil-War policy of exempting slave-owning young men from service while drafting non-slavcowners, this preposterous logic works.

In the Rather case, George W. Bush's service as a fighter pilot in the national guard posed two specific questions:

- Did Bush show up as ordered while he worked on an Alabama political campaign in 1972?
- Why did Bush miss a physical examination resulting in loss of flight status as a jet fighter pilot?

Answers to these questions were never definitively resolved. No one ever proved that Bush was absent-without-leave in summer 1972, as charged by Democratic National Chairman Terry McAuliffe. But Bush aides could not prove that he showed up in Alabama as ordered. Witnesses contradicted one another. The answer depended on where the burden of proof lay. Official records, missing at first but later discovered in the middle of the 2004 electoral campaign, were still confusing. Pentagon records quietly released on the eve of the Democratic National Convention showed that Bush was not paid for the questioned period. That indicates that he did *not* show up. But the Bush people claimed that there was no requirement that he show up. Their official position amounted to this: "He showed up, but if he didn't, it doesn't matter because he didn't have to."

In a key interview after Rather had joined the controversy, he interviewed Mary Karr Knox, secretary for Bush's now deceased commander, Colonel Jerry Killian. Some controversial memos, allegedly written by Colonel Killian, had become the central issue in the controversy. These memos alleged that Bush had received preferential treatment.

Colonel Killian's secretary, however, denied that she had typed these memos. They contained improper terminology, which, according to Mrs. Knox, belonged to the Army, not to the National Air Guard. She accordingly denied typing the memos.

Mrs. Knox did, however, state that she had typed a similar memo, expressing her boss's concern about Bush's preferential treatment. "He was upset about it," said Mrs. Knox. "And that was one of the reasons why he wrote –– well, he wrote the –– memo directing him (i.e., Bush) to take the physical." According to Mrs. Knox, Colonel Killian (charged) Bush with a belief that he could flout the rules and that his fellow officers resented his cavalier attitude.

A gift to the troglodytes

Without the dubious memos this interview would have been devastating for Bush. But Mrs. Knox's extensive comments on Bush's flouting of the rules were ignored in the heat-laden controversy about the false memos. Rather's story was totally consistent. If he had not mentioned the controversial memos, and based his report solely on Mrs. Knox's recollections, the debate would probably have focused on Bush's lack of military service instead of Rather's credibility and reputation. As Rather reported in the same broadcast, "Those who have criticized aspects of our story have never criticized the heart of it, that George Bush received preferential treatment to get into the National Guard and, once accepted, failed to satisfy the requirements of his service."

The red herring worked perfectly for the Bush-Rove team. The flawed messenger became the issue. It was another triumph for Rove. The candidate who dodged the military draft and ducked combat in Vietnam became an unjustly accused martyr. Kerry, the decorated Vietnam hero, became the cowardly liar.

The eternal scapegoat

As the Rather scapegoating spectacularly demonstrates, the red-herring technique is a great political weapon, successfully exploited in the past and destined for further exploitation. Throughout Bush 43's administration, the hackneyed "kill-the-messenger" attacks on the allegedly liberally biased press diverted attention from reported facts about the administration's lies used to justify the Iraq War. Press reports about the notorious Downing Street memo, dated July 23, 2002, proved that the Bush Administration had already decided "to remove Saddam Hussein through military action" at least eight months before the U.S. military invaded Iraq. The all-purpose Bush red herring about the lying liberal press killed this story for the few Bush adherents who even knew about these damning reports.

Rather's scalp signified a great victory for Republican ideologues. They had sought revenge for 30 years, since Rather's reporting on the Watergate scandal culminating in President Nixon's resignation. But Rather's scalp was not enough for the kooky talk-show host Michael Savage (originally Weiner, before he adopted his fierce new cognomen to enhance his reputation as a pundit to be reckoned with). While the controversy was still boiling, Savage asked his radio audience for an answer to this question: "Should Dan Rather be indicted for perjury?"

Savage was obviously referring to Rather's news reports presenting the documents later verified as fraudulent. So far as I know, none of Savage's listeners, estimated in the millions, was alert enough to challenge this ridiculous question. They evidently accepted Savage's implication that what he considers a lie on a television broadcast constitutes perjury. It raises questions not only about Savage's listeners, but also Savage himself. Was he gulling his listeners? Or doesn't he know that only statements made under oath –– for example, in court testimony –– can be the subject of a perjury indictment?

Justice Thomas's straw man

A close relative of the red herring — first cousin, or even sibling — is the straw man. Supreme Court Justice Clarence Thomas provides a classic illustration of this crude technique of changing the subject and deflecting attention from the relevant issue. In an unaccustomed exception to his usual secretive public relations, Justice Thomas spoke to the 1998 National Bar Association convention and made a defenseless straw man of his critics.

Justice Thomas correctly denied that he had come to defend his views. His purpose, he said, was ". . . rather to assert my right to think for myself, to refuse to have my ideas assigned to me as if I was an intellectual slave because I'm black. ... I'm a free man, free to think for myself and do as I please. ... I will not he consigned the unquestioned opinion of others."

As Justice Thomas surely knows, the straw man he flattened had no connection with his critics' condemnation of his judicial philosophy, in which he achieves the remarkable feat of being more reactionary than his colleague Antonin Scalia. Among his many derided decisions is a dissent in the case of a severely beaten prisoner, whose teeth were loosened in the assault. According to Justice Thomas, the prisoner could not base his claim on the Eighth Amendment ban on "cruel and unusual punishment." In cases involving gender bias, Justice Thomas joins with his reactionary colleagues, predictably siding with business interests in these and other instances pitting business against individuals. Along with the reactionary majority, he always votes against campaign-finance limitations, maintaining with Justice Scalia that political campaign donations are somehow transmogrified into "free speech." This contradicts the landmark decision, *Buckley v. Valeo*, in which the justices explicitly denied that campaign contributions were free speech and accordingly upheld limitations on them. (This decision was, of course, overruled in the notorious 2010 *Citizens United* decision.)

It is for these and other politically reactionary aspects of his judicial philosophy that Justice Thomas is condemned by critics, not for his paranoid belief that his political opponents are out to deny his right to decide for himself. Deflecting the discussion away from the relevant issues to the irrelevant claims of persecution reveals Justice Thomas's lack of confidence. Given an opportunity to defend his judicial philosophy before the lawyers' convention, he chose instead simply to attack his critics' motives rather than their complaints about his performance.

Of molehills and mountains

That red herrings and strawmen have a great future in the dumbed-down audience exploited by Fox News and its demagogues is redundantly demonstrated. In the molehill-mountain variant of the red-herring fallacy, the obfuscating critic magnifies a trivial, innocuous statement into an ideological mountain. Supreme Court Justice Sonia Sotomayor's Senate confirmation hearing demonstrates this process. Republican opponents discovered an allegedly damning statement she had made eight years earlier: ". . . I would hope that a wise Latino woman with the richness of her experience would more often than not reach a better conclusion than a white male who hasn't lived that experience." For that innocuous statement, Sotomayor was condemned as a racist by, among others, Rush Limbaugh. During the pre-confirmation process, the Sotomayor statement was quoted by Senator Jefferson Beauregard Sessions III (R, SC) as a sign of her unfitness.

In a rational society, this stretch for a reason to deny a liberal appointee's place on the court would be laughable. Behind it lies the tacit assumption that the predominantly white male justices harbor no cultural prejudices. Moreover, the anti-Sotomayor senators are among the political reactionaries who championed the rejected Reagan appointee, Judge Robert Bork. Among Judge Bork's anti-democratic writings were two scholarly articles condemning a landmark 1965 decision, *Griswold v. Connecticut*. In *Griswold* the court struck down an archaic state law (dating from the nineteenth century) banning doctors' dissemination of birth-control information, even to married couples. According to Judge Bork, the 1965 court's discovery of a constitutional right to privacy in the *Griswold* decision was a heinous violation of the Constitution, which, he claimed, guarantees no such right. Bork took great pride in defending the Connecticut statute regulating private sexual behavior as no different from the government's right to enact smoke-abatement ordinances and generally to regulate actions endangering public health.

In confirming the Sotomayor nomination by a wide margin, the Democratically controlled Senate rolled over the ridiculous molehill-mountain objection. But Fox News's continued commercial success assures the survival of the red-herring fallacy in all its crude disguises.

Is Obama a Muslim, a liar, or both?

According to several polls in late summer, 2010, the incredible number of Americans who believe that President Obama is a Muslim evidently doubled, to as high as 24 percent, and the number of Republicans who believed this lie was 46 percent. This phenomenal change didn't just happen; it was deliberately fomented by the usual suspects, led by master propagandist Rush Limbaugh. His convoluted logic in perpetrating this gigantic lie combined innuendo with a subtle red herring.

Here's how Limbaugh succeeded in making his lie seem plausible to his simple-minded votaries. Assuming an air of benevolent tolerance, Limbaugh said that being a Muslim is fine, just don't lie about it. He thereby transformed the issue. It's not about Obama's being a Muslim; it's about his lying denial that he is a Muslim. Through this subtle red herring, subordinating the basic issue of whether Obama is, in fact, a Muslim to the issue of Obama's integrity, Limbaugh convinced his listeners that this lie is the truth. For if you accept Limbaugh's innuendo that Obama is, in fact, a Muslim, it logically follows that Obama is lying in denying that he is a Muslim. And by simply assuming that Obama is a Muslim instead of providing evidence for this proposition, (the vicious circle fallacy) Limbaugh succeeds in diverting his listeners' attention, thereby facilitating the always easy job of bamboozling his audience with fancy forensic footwork. By presenting his case with this cynically convoluted innuendo-based, red-herring-corrupted "reasoning," Limbaugh can pretend to be an eminently reasonable man, a believer in religious liberty, affronted not by the President's belonging to an alien religion, but by his lying about his true religious identity. It's a classic instance of hypertrophied hypocrisy.

CHAPTER 7

In the Country of the Blind

*". . . A tale told by an idiot Full of
sound and fury, signifying nothing"*

Shakespeare

Hearing a recording of Rush Limbaugh's keynote address to the
Conservative Political Action Committee (PAC) in March, 2009,
I couldn't believe my ears. Before commenting I had to confirm
the message with my eyes — via the Internet-recorded transcript.
Here are his exact words: "We believe that the preamble to the
Constitution contains an inarguable truth: that we are all endowed
by our creator with certain inalienable rights, among them life,
liberty, freedom, and the pursuit of happiness."

What makes this blooper incredible is its appearance in what
the megalomaniacal Limbaugh billed as "my first ever address
to the nation." As head of the pompously fictional Institute for

Advanced Conservative Studies, Limbaugh reflexively pounces on his opponents' trivial mistakes - –– e.g., President Obama's calling the Chicago White Sox stadium "Cominsky" instead of "Comiskey" park. Yet here is this self-proclaimed political genius unable to distinguish between the U.S. Constitution and the Declaration of Independence! The same man who condemns mortgage borrowers for failure to read the fine print in subprime mortgage contracts doesn't even check the Constitution's preamble for reference in a major address.

Mein fuhrer, right or wrong

To Limbaugh's audience his ignorance about our two most important historical documents served not to shake, but to reinforce its faith. Three times during this false reference to the Constitution, Rush's dittoheads interrupted his speech with transcription-noted applause. How should you interpret this preposterous reaction? Were his votaries merely being polite, granting their leader the right to be preposterously wrong? Or do they share their leader's colossal ignorance?

There is another absurd aspect to this incident. As he fearlessly exercised his constitutional right to free speech, Limbaugh warned his auditors that the Obama administration was assaulting his (and their) constitutional rights to free speech. Dittoheads cheered this absurd charge while Limbaugh actively demonstrated its absurdity. Neither before nor after this speech has Limbaugh experienced the slightest effort to abridge his legal right to vent his venomous message.

Limbaugh's blooper on the Constitution was no anomaly. His comments on the West Virginia coal-mining accident, which killed 29 miners in April, 2010, also revealed his habitual contempt for facts. "Where was the miners' union?" demanded Limbaugh, launching into a furious diatribe condemning the alleged union's failure to demand adequate mine-safety precautions. There was, of course, no miners' union to fulfill this presumed duty. But that fact didn't deter Limbaugh from a long-winded denunciation of the mythical union's failure to prevent the tragedy.

Whether his millions of listeners recognized this ludicrous error I have no way of knowing. I have, however, experienced Limbaugh's fans' reactions when you try to confuse them with facts. In one encounter, I corrected a dittohead who blamed Bill Clinton for the assassination of nearly 300 marines in an Islamic radical's suicide bombing in Lebanon. Reacting apoplectically to my reminder that Ronald Reagan, not Bill Clinton, was president when this 1983 marine assassination occurred, the dittohead ended the discussion in a rage, adamantly refusing even to consider the possibility that he could be wrong. And though this may be an extreme instance, it demonstrates our political reactionaries' general determination to preserve erroneous ideological theories despite contradictory facts. Like Fox News viewers who cling to the belief that Saddam Hussein masterminded the 9/11 attacks, or that President Obama was born in Kenya, Limbaugh's fans are impervious to facts that contradict their mythical beliefs.

Lie or mistake?

Limbaugh's demonstrable ignorance can make it difficult to distinguish his lies from honest mistakes. He has a long record of displaying economic ignorance. In April, 2009, when the Commerce Department reported a first-quarter GDP decline of 5.7 percent on an annualized basis, Limbaugh loudly and repeatedly claimed that the GDP had a quarterly 5.7 percent decline. Limbaugh's error is obvious to anyone with even an elementary grasp of government economic data. The 5.7-percent quarterly GDP decline was not the *quarterly* loss; it was the extrapolated *annual* loss based on the quarterly datum. The readily calculated first-quarterly loss based on the 5.7-percent annualized figure was 1.46 percent. Limbaugh had overestimated it by 390 percent. If the first quarter loss had actually been 5.7 percent, as Limbaugh mistakenly claimed, the extrapolated annualized loss would have been a gruesome 21 percent. (These figures are readily calculated via the compound-interest formula, $(1 + r)^n$.)

Limbaugh's quarterly loss mistake was doubtless an honest error. But many of his errors are demonstrable lies. They come in all shapes and sizes — little white lies, big black lies, lies of commission and lies of omission. Limbaugh claims that health costs have doubled under President Obama. Health-care costs have actually stabilized under Obama, to their lowest level in a half century, averaging 4 percent annually vs. 11 percent under Reagan. Limbaugh fabricates lies that no other talk-show would dream of peddling. After President Obama approvingly quoted economic philosopher Adam Smith for his claim that productive work merited decent wages, Limbaugh charged Obama with attacking Smith! Yet his moronic audience accepts these blatant lies as infallible revelations.

In a much bigger, blacker lie, Limbaugh claims that Obama's health-reform legislation establishes "death panels" empowered to require euthanasia for the sick and elderly. This is a sheer fabrication, easily rebutted by simply reading *HR 3200, American's Affordable Health Choices Act of 2009*, Section 1233, Advance Care Planning Consultation. This section provides for advance-care planning for individuals who had not had such planning in the last five years. Consultation included explanation of living wills and durable powers of attorney, health-care proxy's duty, lists of national and state resources, an explanation of end-of-life services, and an explanation of orders about life-sustaining treatment. Section 1233 also requires the Secretary of Health and Human Services to update the annual handbook, *Medicare and You*, with the latest data on the aforementioned services. Nothing in this section remotely suggests "death panels." That charge is merely one of many lies spread by Republican propaganda, notably by Sarah Palin, to inflame their gullible followers.

Lies about the media

Limbaugh habitually lies about what he calls the "driveby media." On his November 18, 2008, broadcast, he told a whopper. The liberal media, he charged, had suppressed the news about former presidential candidate John Edwards's adultery. *The New York Times*, which Limbaugh continually uses as his news source for his uninformed listeners, had run several front-page reports on Edwards's adultery. It was reported on all major news networks.

During the Clinton administration, Limbaugh continually charged The New York Times with being a Clinton house organ. Appearing in a Ted Koppel television interview, Limbaugh said that the Whitewater scandal "would be one of the biggest and most well-kept secrets" if he hadn't reported it. He omitted the damning fact that the *Times* had broken the Whitewater story two years earlier, along with a report on Hillary Clinton's commodities trading.

On his Monday, January 11, 2011, program, Limbaugh broadcast a similar easily rebutted lie –– i.e., that the mainstream media were suppressing news about rising gasoline prices. A Google search of reports produced plenty of reports on rising gasoline prices in the *Times*. "Gasoline Prices Rising to a Two-Year High," was published only a month before Limbaugh's charge. "Rising Gas Prices Have Democrats at Odds," (April 30, 2008); "Gas Prices Send Surge of Riders to Mass Transit," (May 10, 2009); and "Climbing Gas Prices Could Slow a Recovery," (June 8, 2009), all demonstrated the *Times's* commitment to gas-price reporting. But when facts collide with Limbaugh fantasies, the fantasies win.

Reagan's savings-and-loan fiasco

A subject sedulously avoided by Limbaugh and conservatives generally is the late 1980s' savings-and-loan debacle, a 20-year precursor of the 2008 financial meltdown precipitated by the same zealous anti-regulatory policies. Compared with its later counterpart, the S-and-L fiasco was relatively innocuous. It costs taxpayers some $300 billion in current, inflation-corrected dollars, probably 10 percent of the multi-trillion bailout for the subprime mortgage fiasco. It sprang, however, from the same anti-regulatory philosophy championed by Reagan and his politically reactionary follower, George W. Bush.

The incompetence displayed in this Reagan-inspired, 1982 deregulatory legislation is astonishing in its scope. It was mindlessly conceived and carelessly drafted. Before its tardy amendment, the law actually allowed borrowers to bribe an S-and-L official. Auditors were required to report accounting irregularities not to the Federal Home Loan Bank Board (FHLBB), but only to the audited bank. On notification about irregularities, bank officials were supposed to (a) rectify the situation, or (b) turn themselves in. Obedience to the law was voluntary!

Savings-and-loans were also granted special privileges denied to their major competitors, commercial banks. These risk-promoting advantages included a drastically reduced capital/assets ratio, set at 3 percent, half the minimum 6 percent required of commercial banks. The flaccidly lenient 3 percent permitted a savings-and-loan to float a loan volume twice that of a similarly capitalized commercial bank. Moreover, it could count the balance-sheet mush known as "good will" for all of its capital. By 1987, specialists in the voodoo accounting permitted by the 1982 deregulation legislation had inflated the savings-and-loan capital so grossly that "good will" accounted for 45 percent of the industry's total net worth.

Even less excusable than the slovenly drafting of the savings-and-loan deregulation legislation was the stupefying absurdity at its core. The only respectable purpose of the savings-and-loan industry, its sole legitimate reason for being, is to help small homebuyers to get mortgages. Deregulation, however, allowed the industry to drastically *reduce* its loans to small homebuyers. It permitted them to invest in a host of enterprises unrelated to any public purpose whatever — including ski lodges, artwork, junk bonds financing leveraged buyouts, shopping centers, land speculation, and other development projects for which savings-and-loans aren't needed.

Long after the deregulated industry was on a collision course with financial disaster, Congress and the Reagan administration remained asleep. Freed from both regulatory control and marketplace discipline, a new breed of savings-and-loans turned the formerly legitimate industry into a gigantic gambling racket financed by taxpayers.

Their tactics displayed both ingenuity and audacity. Want to circumvent the law banning loans to bank owners? Cycle loans through an obfuscating loop of dummy corporations ending with the owners, suitably disguised. Want to inflate a fraudulent loan? Bribe an appraiser to bloat the property's appraised value. Need to qualify an unqualified borrower? Get him a partner with a healthy financial statement, a practice known as "kissing the paper." Need a deceptive balance sheet to hold regulators at bay? Hire a specialist in voodoo accounting.

With the S-and-L fiasco as a blatant warning, the subsequent far greater subprime mortgage fiasco was an inexcusably greater folly, attributable to the same reckless deregulatory philosophy that produced the S-and-L fiasco. Led by Limbaugh and other reactionary propagandists, who suppressed all mention of the S-and-L debacle, the resulting amnesia permitted the 2008 financial meltdown. President George W. Bush adamantly refused to crack down on reckless mortgage-lending policies that made a warm body the sole qualification for mortgages doomed from the outset to default. Instead of blame for its horrible precedent in the S-and-L fiasco Reagan's Supply-side economics gets praise in a quasi-religious epiphany by Limbaugh and his ideological colleagues.

Meltdown scapegoat

Limbaugh has a preposterous, simple-minded explanation for the subprime mortgage fiasco. It was the government's fault: *over-regulation*, not *under-regulation*. Specifically, Limbaugh blamed the 1977 Community Reinvestment Act (CRA) for the 2008 financial meltdown. He never explains how legislation enacted 31 years earlier could have had such a delayed reaction. And he ignores both the reason for the CRA's enactment and recent events that identify the true cause.

The 1977 CRA was enacted to prevent the then-prevalent mortgage lenders' practice of redlining local maps around minority dwelling places, thereby denying mortgages for houses located within the red-lined districts. Under the CRA, banks caught redlining could be prosecuted. Limbaugh falsely claimed that the CRA forced mortgage brokers to accept minority borrowers who couldn't repay their loans. According to Limbaugh, it was the government, yielding to blacks' political pressure, that was responsible for reckless lending practices.

This racist propaganda was the exact contradictory of the truth. It was the mortgage lenders who exploited black and Hispanic mortgage borrowers, not, as Limbaugh claims, the reverse. In December, 2011, the Justice Department announced history's largest residential fair-lending settlement, a $335-million liability award against Bank of America's Countrywide financial unit, for discriminating against 200,000-plus minorities who were charged higher fees and interest rates than comparable white borrowers posing the same credit risk. Countrywide also steered more than 10,000 minority borrowers into costly subprime mortgages. White borrowers with similar credit ratings received much cheaper, standard loans.

In a lie by omission, Limbaugh predictably ignored this story. It demolishes his hypothesis of the government-sponsored CRA cause for the subprime mortgage fiasco. Never let the dittoheads get confused by the facts. It's the open secret of Limbaugh's success as history's highest paid professional liar.

Economics 000

Limbaugh's economic ignorance is spectacularly exhibited in his January, 2009, newsletter, long after the impending financial disaster was evident to anyone of elementary economic sophistication. "U.S. economy to avoid recession in 2008 due to surprising economic growth," proclaimed the clueless Limbaugh; " . . . after years of EIB (Excellence in Broadcasting), you know, this is America, where it only gets better." Economic growth in

2008 was negative 2.7 percent, its worst performance in nearly a century.

As the Republican Party's chief hatchet man, calling his Democratic enemies socialists, Communists, Marxists, and Fascists, Limbaugh shows that he is as bad at history as he is at prognostication. By every basic measure of economic performance — GDP growth, employment growth, stock-market profits, and federal debt control — Democrats are evidently better capitalists than Republicans, and by overwhelming margins.

Here are the basic economic facts: Over the past six decades, annual GDP growth per capita has risen 70 percent faster under Democrats than under Republicans (2,78 percent vs. 1.64 percent) In the past half century, employment has grown at a 75 percent higher average annual rate under Democrats than under Republicans. Stock-market profits show even greater disparity favoring Democrats. Since the Coolidge presidency, starting 1925, the S & P stock index has grown at a 13 percent average annual rate under Democrats, more than twice the Republicans' 6 percent rate.

In his most incessantly repeated falsehood, a lie perpetually hammered into blockhead skulls, Limbaugh and his Republican colleagues claim that cutting taxes for the wealthiest Americans always increases federal revenue. In his March, 2008, newsletter, Limbaugh credits the Bush tax cuts with "revenue increases."

This ideological fantasy is decisively contradicted by the statistical facts. In the post-World-War-II era, federal debt skyrocketed under the two biggest tax cutters. Under Reagan, federal debt increased by 61 percent (from 33 to 53 percent of GDP). Under George W. Bush it increased by some 40 percent. Only one other president, Bush 41, increased federal debt as a percentage of GDP in those six post-war decades. Under Clinton, who raised the top tax rate by 28 percent (from 31 to 39.6 percent) federal revenue surged by 11 percent and federal debt declined 16 percent (from 68 to 57 percent of GDP).

Republicans are understandably silent about their one great economic achievement — a gigantic redistribution of wealth from the poor and middle-classes to multimillionaires. In the past three Republican-dominated decades, incomes for the top .01 percent (average annual $123 million) have increased by nearly 400 percent. That's 30 times the trivial 12 percent in median income. And during this era, when Republicans dominated national politics (abetted by cooperative Democrats), effective tax rates on the rich have fallen by 11 percent.

It is, however, their overall economic failure that presents Limbaugh and his fellow Republicans with their most difficult question: Why do socialistic Democrats do so much better than Republicans at running a capitalist economy?

Down with Evolution

Compared with his colossal ignorance in political history and economics, Limbaugh is even deeper over his head in purely scientific matters. To my knowledge, Limbaugh never discussed the teaching of Evolution on his radio program. He evidently prefers to evade this issue with his mass audience. He is nonetheless on record agreeing with Evangelical Christians in doubting Darwin's scientific validity. In Lev Chavets's Limbaugh-praising biography, *Rush Limbaugh: An Army of One*, Limbaugh parrots the evangelicals' hoariest argument: Evolution can't explain creation!

Stronger evidence of his antipathy for Evolution appears in Limbaugh's May, 2008, newsletter. In a long interview with Ben Stein, producer of the 2008 documentary film, "Expelled: No Intelligence Allowed," Limbaugh allies himself with Stein in every aspect of his extended diatribe against Darwinism. According to Stein, schools' biology departments violate free-speech guarantees when they ban the teaching of Intelligent Design (ID) as an alleged scientific alternative to evolutionary biology.

This argument is, of course, absurd. Teaching a nonscientific alternative to evolutionary biology has nothing to do with *freedom*, and everything to do with *competence*. A biologist who doubts the basic laws of evolutionary biology resembles a physicist who doubts the Second Law of Thermodynamics, a mathematician who doubts Newton's calculus, or a geographer promoting the flat-earth hypothesis. Science does not demand conformity to orthodoxy; it encourages bold, imaginative hypotheses. But without compelling evidence counter to prevailing theories, scientists are not required to reconsider the 18th-century phlogiston explanation of combustion, the 19th-century belief in a cosmic ether, and other historically rejected theories. At some point, scientists leave past battles behind. Aristotle's physics has historic significance only; a professor who wanted to teach it as a valid alternative to Newton's or Einstein's physics would be fired for professional incompetence with no abrogation of his free-speech rights. Moreover, there would be no protests from Evangelical Christian conservative politicians. Physics, at least in its mundane mechanics aspect, does not inspire the emotional opposition inspired by scientific biology.

Stein's argument collapses into total absurdity with his charge that Darwinism constitutes the racist basis for Hitler's Nazism. This kind of argument is common among anti-evolutionists. After sociopathic teenagers Dylan Klebold and Eric Harris massacred 15 persons at their Colobine, Colorado, high school in 1999, former Republican House Minority Leader Tom DeLay blamed Darwinism. According to DeLay, the Columbine massacre occurred ". . . because our school systems teach our children that they are nothing but glorified apes who have evolutionized out of some primordial mud." Limbaugh expressed his sympathy with this kind of fanatical anti-evolutionism in his Stein interview. According to Limbaugh, believers in evolution, ". . . don't even want to be judgmental about Hitler." As usual, he cites no evidence supporting this idiotic lie.

The eyes prove ID?

At the heart of the ID proponents' objection to evolutionary theory is the assumption that it can't explain anything as intricately complex as the human eye. According to proponents, only an intelligent designer can produce a human eye, with its shape-shifting lens, its aperture-adjusting iris, its light-sensitive image surface, and its rapidly shifting spherical housing, transmitting megabytes of data to the visual cortex every second. Such complexity could never have evolved merely through adaptive mutations, say the evangelical anti-evolutionists.

This argument disintegrates when we investigate the eye's physiology more closely. Like its fellow vertebrates' eyes, the human eye contains several defects testifying to its evolutionary origin. As noted by famed biologist Richard Dawkins, an intelligent designer would laugh at the notion that the retina was the product of intelligent design. After penetrating several components of the eye (cornea, aqueous humor, lens, and vitreous humor), light waves impinge on the retina, where photocells (rods for nighttime vision, cones for daylight vision) register electrical impulses in millions of nerve fibers on the retinal surface. If it had been intelligently designed for maximum efficiency, the nerve-fiber wiring, which connects the photocells to the optic nerve, would have been located on the retina's opposite side, away from the light, not on the side facing the light. Light waves impinging on the photocells pass through the interfering latticework of nerve fibers. They inevitably distort and attenuate the light waves. This inefficient "back wiring" characterizes all vertebrates' eyes.

There are other physiological features that contradict the idea of the eye's intelligent design. Blood vessels cross the retina's inner surface, casting light-interfering shadows. And where nerve fibers unite at a single opening in the retina to form the optic nerve, they create a blind spot. A smart engineer designing the eye would have averted all of these inefficient defects. The vertebrate eye is an advanced stage in an evolutionary process, initiated with crude, light-sensitive cells that aided the vertebrates' primitive ancestors in their struggle for survival. Modern genetics explains explains the process, all the way back to blind bacteria from which multi-celled animals evolved a half billion years ago.

What is demonstrated by the human eye's complexity is not intelligent design, but evolutionary adaptation to biological challenges. Like that of its predecessors, the human eye evolved into a complex organ of increasing visual acuity as that increased activity promoted the survival of individuals endowed with it and the extinction of those who lacked it. Our arboreal ancestors had to perform prodigious feats of visual acuity (along with acrobatic agility and coordination) to achieve their precarious existence in the trees. Powerful jungle predators awaited misfits who fell to the ground. Survival of arboreal species required the acute vision provided by natural selection.

Many other evolutionary anomalies contradict the idea of Intelligent Design. Humans' phrenic breathing nerves extend from the skull's base through the chest cavity and diaphragm. This torturous path creates problems. Anything that interrupts the path of these nerves along their excessive length can hamper breathing. If they had been intelligently designed, these nerves would travel a much shorter, less tortuous path, not from the neck, but from a spot near the diaphragm. Unfortunately, we inherited this inefficient design from fishy ancestors with gills closer to the neck. That location is efficient for fish, but not for us.

Bones inherited from or aquatic evolutionary ancestors give us the familiar back pain suffered by hundreds of millions of our fellow men. Our amphibian and fish ancestors didn't walk on two legs. Even carpal-tunnel syndrome can be traced to poorly adapted wrist and hand bones, bequeathed to use in rudimentary from by aquatic ancestors, who never had to type. Multiple defects obvious in so many animal organs all testify to the authenticity of evolutionary biology. Its improvements are limited by its past, unlike products designed by a human, or humanlike, engineer.

In their insistence on a molding intelligence specifying the design of organs and organisms, like an architect designing a building, ID proponents are guilty of the anthropomorphic fallacy — the assumption that God, or some vaguer entity called the Intelligent Designer, works in the same way as a human being fabricating handiwork. It's an attempt to project human characteristics onto the universe. In Genesis, God's sculpting of Adam out of clay is a primitive illustration of the anthropomorphic fallacy; it assumes the existence of a God who works exactly like a human sculptor, but with superhuman skill.

Against the overwhelming scientific progress achieved in evolutionary biology, ID protagonists offer nothing — merely a faith-based conviction that it can't be true. Even when offered grants for experiments demonstrating ID, its proponents never propose an experiment to test ID. This failure is not for lack of encouragement. After inviting ID enthusiasts to submit research proposals for grants, the Templeton Foundation received no takers. It's easy to see why. Try to think of a hypothetical experiment that would demonstrate the validity of ID. To have any meaning it must be falsifiable. No such experiment is practicable.

Anti-science all the way

Limbaugh's antipathy for science was evident in the early 1990s in a precursor of the global-warming issue — the ozone-hole problem. This problem sprang from scientists' discovery that the most popular airconditioning refrigerant, chlorofluorcarbons (CFCs) were chemically destroying stratospheric ozone (O_3) molecules. Ozone molecules absorb solar ultraviolet radiation, thereby limiting uv-induced skin cancer. Restoring this uv-resistance to stratospheric ozone thus required substitution of a less harmful refrigerant, hydroflurocarbons (HFCs) for the ozone-depleting CFCs. Inspired by a worldwide scientific consensus, a CFC ban was instituted. This successful campaign ultimately resolved the Arctic ozone-hole problem, though further problems have recently surfaced.

Limbaugh naturally picked the wrong side of this controversy. Chief opponent of rectifying the ozone hole was a scientific illiterate, Dixie Lee Ray, who denied that CFC molecules could possibly have destroyed atmospheric ozone. Her reasoning betrayed her basic ignorance. CFC molecules, she claimed, were too heavy to rise into the stratosphere, which begins some seven miles above the earth. This absurd claim contradicts the long-established kinetic theory of gases, which explains the homogenous diffusion of atmospheric gases in uniform proportions. If gravity were the dominant factor in apportioning the distribution of its gaseous constituents, the atmosphere would be stratified into two basic layers, a low band of oxygen (molecular weight 32) and a higher band of nitrogen (molecular weight 28). Atmospheric molecules, however, move so fast (average speed around 1,100 mph, and experience so many collisions with other molecules (2 billion per second) that gravity is a trivial factor in their diffusion. Heavy CFC molecules do reach the stratosphere, just like other randomly, fast-moving gaseous molecules. But, of course, trying to explain these elementary scientific facts to Limbaugh would be impossible. He lacks the basic scientific knowledge to comprehend the problem.

The failure of ozone-hole deniers, compared with the success of global-warming deniers, is less a matter of scientific knowledge than the relative ease and the the comparatively cheap cost of solving the ozone-hole problem. It required only the substitution of a more expensive safe refrigerant for a less expensive, hazardous refrigerant.

A bigger problem

Compared with the ozone-hole problem, global warming poses not only a more complex technological, but an overwhelmingly greater political and economic problem. To massive, politically powerful energy companies like Exxon Mobil, global warming poses an economic threat if the world mounts a serious effort to control it. As a natural consequence, these threatened companies have directed their vast wealth and political power to denigrate the science and obstruct meaningful efforts to obstruct solutions.

Global warming has a ready scientific explanation. Atmospheric greenhouse gases –– notably, carbon dioxide from automobile tailpipes, power plants and other energy-consuming sources –– are steadily increasing with worldwide industrialization (think China). The earth's atmosphere is transparent to high-frequency, high-energy solar radiation, beamed from the sun's 11,000-degree Fahrenheit surface. Diatomic molecules –– oxygen and nitrogen, which comprise 99 percent of the earth's atmosphere –– are transparent to low-frequency heat radiation emitted by the earth's surface.

But the increasing quantities of carbon dioxide and other greenhouse gases are opaque to low-frequency heat energy re-radiated from the earth. British physicist John Tyndale discovered this property of greenhouse gases two centuries ago. Triatomic molecules absorb low-grade heat energy in the same way that glass traps heat energy in greenhouses.

This ever-increasing trapped heat energy is slowly raising average earth temperatures. The following consequences are already observable:

- melting of polar glaciers
- shrinkage of permafrost zones
- coastal flooding
- migration of disease zones
- migration of insect and animal habitats
- intensification of extreme weather
- ocean acidification
- deterioration of coral reefs

Vastly increased carbon-fuel burning has increased worldwide concentrations of carbon dioxide by some 40 percent since 1850. (Annual increments appear in annually recorded content in Hawaii's Moana Loa, a remotely ideal location to measure world carbon-dioxide levels.) Quantitative facts about the expanded production of carbon dioxide explain its huge increase. Accelerated worldwide expansion of automobile ownership, to more than 1 billion in 2011, explains much of the accelerated growth in greenhouse gases. A typical automobile annually burns about 4,000 pounds of gasoline, but it emits at least three times as much carbon dioxide. (The gasoline carbon produces 3.7 times its pre-combustion weight in atmospheric carbon dioxide. Carbon dioxide's molecular weight is 44, 12 for the carbon, another 32 for the two atmospheric atoms).

How can we attribute global temperature rise to hydrocarbon burning? Here's the scientific logic. While the troposphere (lowest seven miles of atmosphere) has warmed over the past half century, the stratosphere has cooled. This increased troposphere-stratosphere temperature difference points to human-caused global warming. Excess carbon dioxide retains more infra-red heat energy re-radiated from the earth's surface, thus shielding the stratosphere from this transferred heat. Stratospheric heat loss balances tropospheric heat gain. If global warming was caused exclusively by intensified solar radiation, an explanation often advanced by global-warming deniers, temperature would rise in both troposphere and stratosphere, for there would be no intensification of tropospheric heat absorption resulting from increasing greenhouse gas. As part of their basic technique of obfuscation, global-warming deniers never allow the discussion to get this deep into technical details.

Limbaugh totally ignores the science behind global warming. He makes no attempt to refute it, because he doesn't know enough even to discuss the technical details, much less refute them. He also denies the authenticity of the scientifically observed consequences of global warming - glacial melting, rising sea levels, etc. Against the virtually unanimous opinion (some 98 percent) of the world's climatologists from 113 nations, we have the deniers, commercial interests, and conservative think tanks like the American Enterprise Institute, which offers $10,000 to scientists who will raise objections to the Intergovernmental Panel on Climate Change (IPCC) reports. Some global-warming deniers have huge conflicts of interest. Arizona State University climatologist Robert Balling reportedly received $800,000 from fossil-fuel companies between 1989 and 2002. But even Prof. Balling balks at the Limbaugh claim that global warming is a hoax. Human activity may play a role in global warming, admits Prof. Balling, and he feels that engineering solutions can be found.

Mountains from molehills

Limbaugh and his fellow global-warming deniers exploit a tremendous forensic advantage. Several years ago, when e-mailed messages from the English climate research unit at the University of East Anglia were publicized, critics seized upon the revelations as evidence of a scientists' conspiracy to falsify data and hoax the public. "Climategate" was allegedly analogous to Watergate, convicting the world's climatologists of the sins revealed in the East Anglia e-mails –– contempt for critics, promulgation of phony data, refusal to divulge sources, and so forth. Climate-science deniers were highly successful in duping the public. In just two years (2008 to 2010) the number of Americans who believed that human-caused global warming was a hoax more than doubled, from 7 to 16 percent.

The global-warming deniers' success stems from their exploitation of a simple-minded propaganda technique long used to subvert sound causes. Darell Kaufman, an earth-sciences professor at Northern Arizona University, describes the tactics:

- First, identify a minor flaw
- Next, attribute this flaw to malicious intent
- Finally, leap to the conclusion that this flaw, no matter how trivial or unrepresentative of the science, disqualifies the entire body of knowledge.

Scientists are almost uniquely inept at defending themselves in public debate. To say that they are reluctant to combat their enemies is vast understatement. For many scientists, it is simply beneath their dignity as scientists to debate their science with political propagandists. The mountain-molehill fallacy is made to order for science deniers. They can take an innocent error, or an irrelevant omission, and make it seem like an earth-shattering revelation of cosmic significance. Anti-evolutionists cite minor gaps in the fossil record as an insuperable refutation of the theory. Combined with innuendo, mountains are erected in simple minds from molehills magnified to gigantic proportions by science deniers. Whereas scientists are deterred from engaging in public debate, Limbaugh exults in anti-scientific agitation, undeterred by any restraints involving his lack of credentials as an anti-science expert, and no qualms about misrepresenting facts.

No scientific consensus?

Lacking enough technical knowledge even to discuss scientific facts, Limbaugh relies on erroneous generalizations about how science is conducted to justify his anti-scientific denials. There is no such thing as a scientific consensus, says Limbaugh. His argument goes like this: Since science is always open to challenge, it can never declare a subject closed. In a limited sense, this is true. Science does not operate like the Catholic Church in its refusal ever to reconsider papal infallibility. Science permits challenges to solidly established scientific theories – for example, to the 19th-century Second Law of Thermodynamics. But perpetual-motion gets skeptical, not enthusiastic, hearings from scientists.

It is easy to find a scientific dissenter to just about any solidly established scientific fact or theory. In 1988, less than a decade after medical scientists had established the human immunodeficiency virus (HIV) as the cause of AIDs, a distinguished biologist, Peter Deusberg, denied the HIV-AIDs causation theory. According to Deusberg, HIV is merely a harmless passenger virus, found by coincidence in patients ill from other causes –– malnutrition, drug abuse, etc. Following Deusberg's advice, South African President Thebo Mbeki denied thousands of AIDs patients the orthodox treatment, thereby condemning them to unnecessary deaths. Deusberg was not a professionally incompetent crackpot. At age 33, he was the first medical biologist to identify a cancer-causing gene. About his denial on the HIV-AIDs causation, colleagues called him "pathologically stubborn," and his dissent is disregarded by orthodox scientists. Contrary to Limbaugh's opinion that a scientific consensus is an oxymoron, scientists have an extremely strong consensus on HIV-AIDs causation. (The real oxymoron would be a scientifically knowledgeable rightwing talk-show host.)

America's most patriotic talk-show host?

Some years ago, on the local KFYI Phoenix radio station, Limbaugh's introduction credited him as "the nation's most patriotic talk-show host." Its sudden abandonment I attribute (a conjecture, not direct knowledge) to increasing knowledge about Limbaugh's draft-dodging during the Vietnam War. All of Limbaugh's biographers, even the Limbaugh-admiring Lev Chavets, admit that Limbaugh's evasion of military service in Vietnam was suspect. According to biographer Paul D. Colford, records indicate that Limbaugh's draft board accepted his doctor's word that he had an inoperable pilonidial cyst. Limbaugh evidently presented his doctor's report to the the draft board which otherwise would have classified him 1A, or at least ordered a military physical exam as a step toward a draft. Regardless, his own failure to serve didn't deter him from attacking Clinton with the prevailing Republican charge of draft-dodging. Questioned before a liberal group why he hadn't served in Vietnam, Limbaugh gave an ironic reply, "I did not want to go, just as Governor Clinton didn't." This quote was not from a hostile biographer, but from the previously noted admiring biographer, Lev Chavets.

The galling thing about Limbaugh's failure to serve is not so much his draft dodging but his self-righteous patriotism and condemnation of better men than he –– notably, the decorated Vietnam vet John Kerry - as unpatriotic. Even worse is his membership in that neoconservative group who measure patriotism by your willingness to sacrifice others' lives in your wars, while you cheer the slaughter from the safety of the sidelines. So successful is Limbaugh is playing the superpatriot that he gets telephone calls from battle-scarred veterans praising his patriotism. They evidently assume that he served in the military.

But no hypocrisy can alienate Limbaugh's docile followers, not even his drug addition episode, in which he beat a doctor-shopping rap by hiring a high-priced lawyer notorious for getting wealthy defendants off. In 2003, Limbaugh was forced to confess, obviously unwillingly, that he was a drug addict, in thrall to the painkiller oxycontin. Even that would not be so bad if Limbaugh hadn't taken a hard line against persons like himself a few years earlier; "Too many whites are getting away with drug use. The answer is to . . . find the ones who are getting away with it, convict them, and send them up the river." But that statement applied to others, not Limbaugh. Moreover, there's no evidence that he lost a single listener as the price of his hypocrisy. He could evidently be convicted of serial child molestation and still emerge with his audience intact.

Limbaugh is reminiscent of Senator Joe McCarthy. Like McCarthy, Limbaugh is no totalitarian threat to America. As it was for McCarthy, publicity, not power, is Limbaugh's goal. McCarthy led American reporters around like Pavlov's dogs responding to clanging bells. He used morning press conferences to announce afternoon conferences at which he would allegedly divulge the names of 47, 51, or 207 State Department communists. No man was ever quicker than this super prevaricator to call opponents liars, said McCarthy's biographer, Richard Rovere. The same is true of Limbaugh, who is just as prolific a liar as McCarthy.

Understanding the Limbaugh cult

Limbaugh's success is duping his gullible audience is readily explained. His overwhelming male, Bible-belt dittoheads display their arrested development when their calls are answered. They are often flattered into stuttering incoherence when they talk with the great "El Rushmo." Limbaugh strokes them with fulsome praise when they bleat back the identical messages he preaches. Limbaugh's dittoheads belong to a gigantic club reminiscent of children's radio programs during the 1930s. You could become a member of Inspector Post's detective club if you mailed in a cereal box top.

Limbaugh appeals to the same juvenile sense of exclusionary belonging. After he played in a jetset golf pro-am, he used to tell his audience all about it. It inspires dittoheads, even those with $50,000 incomes, with the sense that they, too, belong vicariously to the plutocratic elite. They respond to Limbaugh's undisguised racism, evident from such incidents as his broadcasting of "Barack the Magic Negro" and telling a black caller to "take that bone out of your nose and call me back."

Yet despite the never-ceasing bombast, this college dropout, former disk jockey, is evidently a quivering hulk beneath his arrogantly confidently assertive exterior. Chafets publishes a self-pitying e-mail from Limbaugh after his roasting at the 2009 correspondents' dinner: "I know I am a target, and I know I will be destroyed eventually. I fear that all I have accomplished and all the wealth I have accumulated will be taken from me, to the cheers of the crowd. I know I am hated and despised by the American left."

On reading this passage, I felt the same sense of incredulity, if a little less intense, than I felt on hearing Limbaugh confuse the Constitution with the Declaration of Independence (cited at the chapter's beginning). Can this truly be an accurate quote from Limbaugh's biographer? Since this is an authorized biography, with Limbaugh cooperating with his biographer, there's no objective reason to doubt Chavets's word. But these are indeed strange words from a man who ostensibly exults in his enemies' hatred. If Chafets's quote is accurate, Limbaugh's public persona, playing the bravely confident high priest of conservatism, is phonier than anyone could have surmised.

This phony bluster is evident in Limbaugh's repeated boasting about his courage and his constantly charges of his opponents' cowardice. It takes immense courage to issue his charges, as when he called the Georgetown university law student, Sandra Fluke, a "slut," because she defended government-financed contraception. "I'm not going to be silenced," he responds to critics, in self-praising paeans to his indomitable courage.

Then suddenly, after sponsors began cancelling their ads on his show, Limbaugh caved, admitted he "had descended to the level of his opponents," and apologized for his vulgarity. Limbaugh's claim, that he is a courageous disseminator of truth, is a sick joke. And his self-pitying fear that he will ultimately be destroyed by opponents whom he deliberately antagonizes betrays the contemptible psyche of a sentimental megalomaniac, deluded by the same self-promoting bombast he uses to dupe his gullible auditors.

CHAPTER 8

Free-Lunch Patriotism

> *"Patriotism is the last refuge of a scoundrel."*
>
> Samuel Johnson

Fox News commentator Bill O'Reilly's choice of *Pinheads and Patriots* as the title for his 2010 book provides an interesting insight into conservatives' obsession with patriotism. *Pinheads and Patriots* is a false dichotomy, like Lewis Carroll's poem in *Through the Looking Glass:*

> *"The time has come," the Walrus said,*
> *"To talk of many things:*
> *Of shoes — and ships — and sealing*
> *wax —*
> *Of cabbages — and kings."*

If O'Reilly was seeking an intellectual comparison, something like, "Logicians and Pinheads," or "Thinkers and Pinheads" would be more appropriate. If patriotism is the focus, then "Traitors and Patriots" would do better. A pinhead-patriot comparison makes no more sense than Carroll's cabbages-and-king association. But, of course, Carroll wasn't trying to make sense; he was, in fact, deliberately creating nonsense. Through his inappropriate word association, however, O'Reilly was obviously determined to exploit the emotional appeal of patriotism. Like Shakespeare, he acknowledged "the pale cast of thought," resolving to imbue it with the emotional appeal of patriotism.

O'Reilly nonetheless believed the pinhead-patriot association was a brilliant forensic device. Months after his book's publication, he continued its use on his television program. Logic can't compete with emotion in a conservative context.

Patriotism on the cheap

The most astounding aspect of O'Reilly's and other so-called conservatives' concept of patriotism is how cheap it is. Wearing a flagpin is one criterion. Rush Limbaugh denounced Barach Obama for this omission (and characteristically denounced Obama for hypocrisy when he corrected it. Reciting the pledge of allegiance is another vitally important patriotic symbol, highly valued by Tea Partiers.)

In one of their few publicized disputes, former Vice President Dick Cheney accused President Bush of "leaving a soldier on the battlefield." The putative soldier was Cheney's aide, I. Lewis (Scooter) Libby, convicted of perjury in the notorious Valerie Plame Wilson case. To conservatives like Cheney, military service is metaphorical, not actual. Like his boss, Libby was a Vietnam War draft dodger, who never served a day in the military. Cheney was not the only Libby defender to seize on this service metaphor. A *Wall Street Journal* article asserted, "Scooter Libby was a soldier in your –– our –– war in Iraq."

New York Times columnist Paul Krugman fulminated against this military metaphor. "Shuffling papers in an airconditioned Washington office is . . . like putting your life on the line in Anbar or Baghdad. Spending 30 minutes in a minimum security prison, with a comfortable think-tank job awaiting at the other end, is exactly the same as having half your face or both legs blown off by an I.E.D."

"Why Should I Go?"

Though O'Reilly includes himself among the anti-pinhead patriots, he off-handedly acknowledges his own draft-dodging during the Vietnam War, with this bland admission: "Fortunate guys like me could go to college and avoid the draft." This comment reveals an attitude similar to Cheney's. Asked why he ducked military service during Vietnam, Cheney replied, "I had other priorities." This cavalier response suggests that he, Cheney, was, if not unique, at least deserving of special consideration. How many people don't have "other priorities" compared with wartime military service?

Unlike Cheney, however, O'Reilly obviously felt obligated to explain his rejection of military service. For Cheney, Vietnam was "a noble cause," but one that nonetheless was not his responsibility. O'Reilly attempts to justify himself by at least discussing his attitude toward Vietnam. This discussion's superficiality marks him, contrary to his confident egotism, as an incorrigible pinhead.

O'Reilly does acknowledge a historical fact denied, or at best ignored, by conservative defenders of the war. In its latter years, protests multiplied against the injustice of the college draft deferments. Toward the war's end, college deferments were suspended, putting congressmen's and rich family's sons subject to compulsory service. This threat hastened the war's end, as the previously favored escapees from the draft became liable for military service.

But despite his admission of the military draft's inequity, O'Reilly's discussion fails to consider the key issue. He admits his antipathy toward "anti-war zealots –– hotheads, stoned, unwashed zombies." Claiming to listen to both sides of the debate, he pondered such profound questions as these: "Did Americans want to kill babies on purpose?"; "Was the U.S. the Second Coming of the Third Reich?" That was as far as O'Reilly got in examining the basic issues. He totally ignores the critical question: Why did the U.S. intervene in Vietnam's civil war? He ignores President Lyndon Johnson's Gulf-of Tonkin-resolution, based on a fabricated charge that a North Vietnamese ship attacked a U.S. warship. He ignores President Johnson's and then President Nixon's reasons for continuing the needless sacrifice –– i.e., to avoid being history's first war-losing president. To anyone with any historical knowledge, the first war-losing president was James Madison, whose War of 1812, by any rational assessment, was won by the British.

For his opinions about the war, O'Reilly relied not on facts, but on instincts. ("My country was under assault from all directions, and *my instinct* [italics added] was that much of it was unfair." He has no criticism of Vietnam hawks, those who propounded the ultimately demolished domino theory. This domino theory predicted a Cold War defeat if we were defeated in Vietnam. But contrary to the Vietnam hawks, we lost in Vietnam and won the Cold War. North Vietnam's victory had no effect on the Cold War. The Soviet Union finally collapsed in the rubble of its abysmal economic incompetence. The question of why we entered the Vietnam War and the hawks' abysmally wrong analysis evidently means nothing to O'Reilly.

Strange logic

There is a strange logic, more accurately termed illogic, in conservatives' attitudes toward draft dodgers. With their incessant harping on patriotism, you would think they would judge draft dodgers harshly. They do partially fulfill this expectation. They judge *Democratic* draft dodgers harshly. But they generally exempt Republican draft dodgers from all criticism. Conservatives allow you to cheer the slaughter from sideline safety, provided you support a war. Patriotism is judged not by your willingness to risk *your* life, but by your willingness to risk *others* lives.

I learned this anomalous fact by questioning conservatives about Cheney's draft dodging. As the overwhelming response to this question, responding conservatives counter with Bill Clinton's draft dodging. While tacitly condoning Cheney's draft dodging, they unanimously denounce Clinton's. As previously noted, Cheney enthusiastically supported the Vietnam War, whereas Clinton vehemently opposed it. Here is the conservative position: If you support a war, you can refuse to fight it, and still be a patriot. If you oppose the war, however, you are patriotically obligated to fight it.

There is, however, another curious anomaly about defenders of Cheney's draft dodging. Those who have served are always quick to point out *their* military service, especially if they are combat veterans. They hold themselves to a much higher patriotic standard than they set for their political leaders, while judging their political opponents by the same high standard that they set for themselves. This indicates to me a refusal to confront facts, a proclivity observable in every aspect of conservative political behavior. Christian evangelicals pursue a similar double standard in their sexual morality. Despite their family-values rhetoric, they absolve serial adulterer Newt Gingrich of his sexual transgressions, as well as his Vietnam draft dodging, while holding Bill Clinton guilty on both counts.

Conservative draft dodging produced many bizarre justifications contrary to normal logic. Let's start with this reasonable premise: if you believe in a war, you should be willing to fight it. Don't use this logic on the uniquely corrupt former Republican House Majority Leader, Tom DeLay (R, TX). At the 1988 Republican National Convention, when Vice Presidential candidate Dan Quayle was under fire for ducking military service in Vietnam, DeLay called a press conference to explain. When they dodged the military draft, both he (DeLay) and Quayle were making an altruistic sacrifice, explained DeLay. They magnimously sacrificed their opportunity to serve in Vietnam so that two minority men (presumably black or Hispanic) could exploit the economic opportunity afforded by military service. (One reporter who heard this bizarre excuse allegedly inquired, "Who is that nut?")

Less bizarre, but no less irrational than DeLay's draft-dodging excuse, was Christopher Buckley's mea-culpa admitting his guilt at having ducked the draft via a medical subterfuge. Happily liberated from his father's (William F. Buckley's) political and religious conservatism, son Christopher nonetheless demonstrated that his liberation was only partial, at least when he wrote his article 30 years ago. Totally ignoring the reasons for fighting the Vietnam War, the younger Buckley saw it as a patriotic test of virility. He and other Vietnam draft dodgers should have served only to demonstrate their patriotism, not for dedication to a worthwhile cause. In Buckley's words, "I should have gone, if only to bear witness."

The Nixon heritage

There's a long list of Vietnam draft dodgers, who overwhelmingly backed the Iraq War, which they were, of course, too old to fight. The second Bush administration was infested with them: Supreme Court Associate Justice Samuel Alito; high-ranking Pentagon officials, Paul Wolfowitz and Douglas Feith; former UN Ambassador, John Bolton; Pentagon adviser, Richard Perle; and naturally, Bush's political guru, Karl Rove, who also made sure that his young, military-age son didn't join the military.

Rove masterminded Bush's 2004 electoral campaign by turning the tables on Democratic candidate John Kerry, a thrice-decorated Vietnam veteran. Rove made Kerry the unpatriotic candidate vs. the draft-dodging President. He learned his brand of gutter politics from masters like the late Lee Atwater. This was the Nixon era, just prior to Watergate, when the rampant corruption and totalitarian practices set a precedent for the Bush 43 administration. In the 1972 Presidential campaign, when Rove was a sophomore in Nixon's school for political corruption, the Nixon people used tactics later expanded by Rove in Bush's service. Nixon had unleashed his assistant, H.R. Haldemann, a draft dodger in both World War II and Korea, to attack Democratic candidate, George McGovern, a decorated bomber pilot in the World War II European theater. According to Haldemann, McGovern was unpatriotic at best, traitorous at worst, for his opposition to Nixon's Vietnam policy. This benighted Nixon-Kissinger policy sacrificed an additional 25,000 Americans in a losing cause made worse by dragging out an ignominious withdrawal. And in a perfect parallel with Bush's Iraq War, Republican congressmen's sons almost totally escaped military service in Vietnam.

Rising rapidly in the Republican hierarchy to his post as chief adviser to President Bush, Rove took on the job of attacking Democratic war veterans, especially decorated veterans, as unpatriotic. Rove's fingerprints are all over the nefarious 2002 Georgia senatorial race. Rove had a natural affinity, as well as political fraternity, with fellow Vietnam draft dodger, Saxbe Chambliss, who defeated incumbent Senator Max Cleland, a triple-amputee from service in Vietnam. The key to this campaign was a televised ad showing Cleland as Osama bin Laden and Saddam Hussein. As its unmistakable implication, this doctored photograph portrayed the wounded Veteran as a traitor, and by innuendo, his draft-dodging opponent as a patriot. It's a brand of gutter politics that works in erstwhile rebel territory, historically notorious for perverse rules of military service. (During the Civil War, slave owners with more than 20 black chattels were exempt from military service. It was the duty of poor, non-slaveholder whites to defend the slaveowners' decadent way of life!)

The reversal of patriotic roles in the 2002 senate race encouraged Rove for the 2004 Presidential campaign. It had a parallel situation, a Republican draft dodger running against a wounded, decorated Vietnam veteran. False propaganda from the misnamed Swiftboat Veterans for Truth attacked John Kerry, who foolishly allowed the attacks to go unanswered until their negative impact was solidly established. Again, the Republicans reversed the normal situation, which in a battle of patriotic propaganda would favor military heroes over draft-dodging opponents.

There were historic lessons from the past ignored by the Democrats. In North Carolina's 1986 senatorial campaign, incumbent Republican James Broyhill launched a last-minute attack on his Democratic opponent, charging him with "lacking courage in national defense." Broyhill's cheap shot boomeranged. His opponent, former state governor Terry Sanford, a decorated paratrooper in World War II, countered by publicizing Senator Broyhill's non-existent military record. Evidently shocked that his opponent would retaliate, Broyhill feebly spluttered excuses about how his medical problems prevented his service during the Korean War. It was a political TKO in the final electoral round. Even in the era of free-lunch economics, free-lunch patriotism can sometimes lose.

Another absentee in the Korean War was the notorious Norman Podhoretz, a neoconservative called by former Village Voice columnist Jack Newfield, "the most bloodthirsty intellectual since Tamerlane." Draft-age during the war, Podhoretz ducked military service in favor of literature studies at Columbia and Cambridge. Despite his refusal to risk his life, Podhoretz courageously risks others' lives in his favored wars –– Vietnam, Iraq, and, if he had his way, Iran.

Podhoretz's war lust has no rational basis. He was a dedicated believer in the domino theory, falsely linking a defeat in Vietnam to a defeat in the Cold War. He has never acknowledged this error despite the proof provided by subsequent events: We lost in Vietnam, but won the Cold War, a direct refutation of the domino theory.

The public revolt against the injustice of the college draft deferments during Vietnam led ultimately to abolition of the military draft, supplanted by an all-volunteer force. Hopes for voluntary military service as an antidote to the draft's inequities have waned as the superannuated Afghan and Iraq Wars have exacted mercilessly inordinate sacrifice from U.S. troops forced to endure multiple duty tours in those incredibly hostile environments. Some former advocates for the draft's abolition now advocate its renewal as a means of spreading the sacrifice evaded by the general population. In the weekly casualty reports, the concentration of grossly disproportionate sacrifice borne by poor, rural, small-town Americans was glaringly obvious. In view of the outrageous origin of the Iraq War, the brazen lies told by Bush and Cheney in justification of corrupt ventures conducted with such stupefying incompetence, it is astonishing that our soldiers accept the traumatic ordeal of life in such unimaginable conditions. The soldiers' and their families' stoic acceptance is highlighted by the manner used by Bush-Cheney to make war acceptable for the overwhelming majority of Americans, for whom these wars are free of all visible sacrifice. Even its financial cost was hidden, deleted from the official budget deficit.

"Marine Wedding"

An incongruous *New York Times* society-section article, with a stark photograph laconically labeled "Marine Wedding," dramatically exhibited the vast gulf separating the sacrificial victims of President Bush's Iraq war and the coddled beneficiaries of his enriched plutocracy. Under normal circumstances, this photograph would never qualify for publication in the *Times* society section, which normally publishes only photographs of the newly wedded rich. "Marine Wedding" was photographed in a rural Illinois town, not far in geographical distance, but lightyears in cultural distance from the purlieus of the privileged.

What distinguishes "Marine Wedding" from the dependably beaming euphoric faces of the society page is the blank expression of the newly weds. The young bride stares bleakly ahead with a deadpan, joyless look of querulous gravity. In full dress, battle-decorated, purple-hearted uniform, the marine bridegroom is necessarily expressionless, his white, reconstructed face a noseless, chinless pullover mask. This "face" represents a modern medical marvel, one of the many that have reduced fatalities by some 70 percent since the Vietnam War. While serving in Iraq, Sergeant Ty Ziegel was trapped in a burning truck hit by a suicide bomber. The fiery blast demolished his face and shattered his skull.

Nineteen surgeries left him a masklike face reconstructed from salvaged tissue, with holes replacing his missing nose and ears, and a plastic dome replacing his shattered skull. The publication of "Marine Wedding" reminded me of the roughly contemporaneous announcement of former President Bush's daughter, Jenna Bush's, engagement to Henry Hager, a young man who would never be caught alive or dead in a military uniform. Hager fittingly worked for Karl Rove, another architect of the needless war that produced the disfigured marine and thousands more like him.

Former President Bush's idea of sacrifice was humorously (in the sick sense) revealed in a January 16, 2007, interview on the Lehrer News Hour. Asked why, if the War on Terror was such a fearful threat to the nation, he never asked the public to make any sacrifice, the President responded in a way that made his previous inanities appear relatively innocuous. ". . . I think a lot of people are in this fight. I mean they sacrifice peace of mind when they see the terrible injuries of violence on television every night." That quote revealed more than mere stupidity. It showed that the former President was barely half conscious.

In the 2012 presidential campaign candidate Mitt Romney maintained free-lunch patriotism as a Republican principle. A Vietnam draft-dodger himself, who spend months in Paris as a Mormon missionary, Romney had justified his five sons' rejection of military service during the Iraq and Afghanistan wars because they had demonstrated their patriotism by working in his 2008 presidential campaign. But his and his sons' lack of military service didn't deter him from playing the patriotic card, talking tough about possible war against Iran and otherwise threatening military action instead of President Obama's more diplomatic approach. It's the constant Republican expression of patriotism: the willingness to sacrifice others' lives in pursuit of partisan goals.

CHAPTER 9

The Supreme Court Plutocrats

"Corporate expenditures for political purposes ... have supplied one of the principal sources of corruption in our political affairs."

Theodore Roosevelt
1910

Former President George W. Bush's catastrophic eight-year tenure plunged the United States into such deep thickets that it will take more than a decade to extricate ourselves. Bush's half-hearted effort in Afghanistan and the absurd war in Iraq, based on Vice President Dick Cheney's lie that Saddam Hussein plotted the 9/11 terrorist attacks, have cost well over a trillion dollars and thousands of mutilated or dead bodies. The massive deregulatory policies that produced the 2008 financial meltdown demonstrated Bush's economic incompetence fully equal to his military incompetence. But even these twin catastrophes may prove less durable than his disastrous appointments, the politically reactionary justices John Roberts and Samuel Alito, to the Supreme Court. These appointments created an ultra-conservative majority whose 5-4 decisions will doubtless continue to move our judicial system back toward the robber-baron plutocracy of the 1880s, erasing gains made during the 20th century. And this ultraconservative domination could extend far into the future.

Justice Antonin Scalia, in particular, is devoted to ultraconservative illogic. As justification for his predictable vote against extending the Voting Rights Act, a vital necessity to prevent Republican voter suppression chiefly in the erstwhile Confederacy, Justice Scalia referred to the safeguarding of minority voting *rights* as the "perpetuation of racial *entitlements*." Justifying his vote against the Affordable Health Care Act, he cited an absurd slippery-slope argument –– that it could lead to the government's requiring people to buy brocolli.

In their typically close 5-4 rulings, these ultraconservative justices are seldom guided by any respectable judicial philosophy, but chiefly by the reactionary political goals of revoking constitutional gains achieved under previous courts –– notably, the 1960s' Warren court. Justices Scalia and Thomas have demonstrated that they can't even abide by common-sense ethical requirements. They flaunt their offenses as if they stood above the standards generally demanded of judges. And their philosophy of Originalism, which depicts our founders as numbskills who believed that they could write a perfect constitution, to be interpreted in the light of late-eighteenth-century political philosophy throughout eternity, is a humorless joke. Jefferson once opined that the Constitution be rewritten every 25 years.

Freedom or license?

In the last major case of 2010-2011, Justice Scalia displayed his superficial approach to logic. In his majority opinion for this case, *Brown v. Entertainment Merchants Association*, Justice Scalia attempted to justify nullification of a California law restricting the sale of violent video games to minors. Justice Scalia defended violent video games because ". . . they communicate ideas — and even social messages" deserving of First-Amendment, free-speech protection. He rejected the argument that violence was like obscenity, which, he agrees, lacks free-speech protection. "Disgust" at violence "is not a valid basis for restricting expression," wrote Justice Scalia. But what justifies legal bans on obscenity if not disgust? And does gratuitous, mindless violence, graphically depicted in violent video games, "communicate ideas" more important than pornography? Along with the majority of justices, Scalia dismissed studies correlating the viewing of violent videos with youthful aggression as "unpersuasive." He didn't explain how obscenity differs from violence. Even Justice Thomas rejected Scalia's reasoning.

Justice Thomas, however, preserved his reputation as a biased ideologue in an earlier decision, *Connick v. Thompson*. The sloppily reasoned *Brown* decision is positively brilliant compared with the outrageous *Connick v. Thompson* decision. In *Thompson*, Justice Thomas justified the nullification of a $14-million jury award to a murder-charge defendant (i.e., John Thompson) who had been falsely imprisoned for 18 years because prosecutors had destroyed exculpatory evidence proving the convicted defendant's innocence. Thompson was robbed of 18 years of life by corrupt prosecutors — and then robbed of his just restitution by five "conservative" Supreme Court justices.

Here are the undisputed facts, accepted by the justices in Thompson's case. One month before his scheduled execution, a private investigator discovered that New Orleans prosecutors had violated the Constitution by withholding exculpatory evidence from Thompson's defense lawyers. Prosecutors withheld police reports, witness statements, and audio tapes, including proof that the crime-scene blood was not Thompson's. After this exculpatory evidence was revealed, Thompson was retried for murder. A jury took only 35 minutes of deliberations to acquit, and Thompson was awarded $14 million in damages for the prosecutors' theft of 18 years of life.

In this inexcusably unjust decision, the five "conservative" justices demonstrated their contempt not only for elementary justice, but for a prior landmark 1963 court decision, *Brady v. Maryland*, in which the court ruled that the Constitution requires prosecutors to give exculpatory evidence to the defense. Writing for fellow dissenters (Breyer, Kagan, and Sotomayor), Justice Ruth Bader Ginsburg demolished Thomas's majority opinion. Thomas argued that the New Orleans DA couldn't be held liable because the violation of the Brady decision was "aberrant," not a systematic denial of the Brady requirement to give defense attorneys all exculpatory evidence. Justice Ginsburg cited the voluminous damning evidence at Thompson's retrial as proof that the prosecutors had indeed systematically violated Brady and, consequently, the Constitution. That four of the other "conservative" justices would agree in this travesty testifies to their judicial incompetence as well as their ideological activism. No Supreme Court in the past century has had five justices who don't believe in justice.

Consolidating plutocracy

In their landmark decision, *Citizens United v. Federal Election Commission*, these same five justices abolished a full century of campaign-finance laws designed to curb the Gilded-Age robber barons' power to corrupt the political process by buying congressmen's votes. One overturned law, barring corporate financing of federal legislation, was signed by President Teddy Roosevelt in 1907. This Tillman Act was a response to the 1996 election of William McKinley, who overwhelmed his Democratic opponent, William Jennings Bryan, with corporate money.

At the intellectual roots of this decision are two so-called "legal fictions." These are metaphysical constructs fabricated by lawyers to justify ridiculous legal doctrines when they can't think of anything better. According to one legal fiction, money –– i.e., a political campaign donation -- is equivalent to free speech. In the other, an even more ludicrous concept, the court defined corporations as human beings, endowed with the same civil rights -- i.e., free speech -- as individual citizens.

The triumphant justices obviously ignored their decision's logical implications. If money is free speech, how can courts ban monetary contributions to judges or jurors by parties to lawsuits, or even defendants in criminal trials? According to the court's logic, mere involvement in a judicial proceeding should pose no obstacle to your First Amendment right to free speech. If money is free speech, judicial anti-bribery statutes should be declared unconstitutional. Free speech, in the court's opinion, is a sacred right, not to be nullified to serve less important goals.

In their *Citizens United* decision, the conservative justices also flouted a previous Supreme Court's denial of the legal fiction equating money with free speech. In the 1976 *Buckley v. Valeo decision*, the court ruled that campaign donations were *not* free speech and thus could be limited. But, of course, the Roberts court could not allow common sense to demolish a legal fiction that serves their plutocratic political philosophy.

In his ruling opinion, Justice Kennedy argued that you can't prove campaign donations buy legislators' votes. The legal briefs, he asserted, contained no evidence that campaign donations bought even one legislator's vote. This claim indicates either (a) that the legal briefs ignored overwhelming statistical evidence correlating money with votes, or (b) that Justice Kennedy was born yesterday. In my book, *Cleaning Out Congress: The Case for Term Limits*, I cite voluminous statistical evidence correlating campaign contributions with votes. Instances could be multiplied indefinitely, and I doubt that anyone can produce any negative statistical correlation -- i.e., instances in which a majority of congressmen voted against their donors' interests.

Here are a few representative examples demonstrating that campaign contributions are simply legalized bribery. In a vote on U.S. maritime legislation in the mid-1970s, congressmen voting for the maritime industry (ship owners and maritime labor union) received more than 10 times as much in PAC contributions from maritime interests as the small minority of opponents (an average $2,700 vs. $200) By a vote of 31-5, the House Merchant Marine and Fisheries Committee sponsored a cargo-preference bill that required 9.5 percent of imported oil to be transported in American ships. To the maritime industry, this bill delivered a huge, multimillion-dollar subsidy. To oil consumers, it meant some $3 billion in higher gas and heating oil prices.

Other deniers that campaign donations buy votes make a ludicrous logical error. Attempting to rebut a classic case of vote bribery, the late columnist James K. Kilpatrick argued that because a tiny minority voted against their donor's interest, that fact proved that campaign donations don't buy votes. In other words, unless *all* the recipients vote for a donor's interest, you must assume that the donations had *no* influence. Actually, the reverse is true. If just *one* vote is bought, the legislative process is corrupted to some degree. Especially in the U.S. Senate, where there are only 100 members, the purchase of one vote can corrupt the entire process, producing passage of a bill that would otherwise have been defeated.

Denying that campaign contributions ever buy votes also shows an abysmal ignorance of the concept conflict of interest. Consider a truly blatant conflict of interest, yet nonetheless analogous to a congressmen's receipt of political contributions and voting his donor's interest. Consider the case of a father serving as a juror in the criminal murder trial of his son. Who would believe the father's claim that he could serve on such a jury without allowing his parenthood to influence his decision? Yet there is no way to prove it necessarily would. We simply know from experience that there are countless instances in which personal interest corrupts judgment. For several decades after cigarette smoking was linked with lung cancer, heart disease, and emphysema, the tobacco industry's hired guns challenged the damning Public Health Service data as scientifically unfounded. Six-figure salaries induce people to lie when their employers' interest, and consequently their own, require them to lie. The tobacco industry didn't pay its experts to give unbiased scientific opinions. It paid them to fog the issue in an effort to sustain cigarette sales and industry profits. To hell with their effect on smokers' health. Yet the proof that Justice Kennedy demands to establish the purchase of votes by big corporations is lacking also in the prostitution of scientific experts hired to deny cigarettes' health hazards. Congressmen are corrupted in the same way that tobacco-industry experts were corrupted by their employers' interest in perpetrating scientific lies.

In moments of inadvertent candor, congressmen themselves admit their corruption. Former Senate Majority Leader, Mississippi's Trent Lott, resorted to overt extortion. Soliciting businessmen's donations, Lott said, "By failing to act today, you lose a unique chance to be included in legislative policy debates that will affect your business" The difference between Lott and other corrupt congressmen open to corporate bribery is merely Lott's inadvertent candor.

Compounding the logical problems posed by the money-equals-speech metaphor, treating a corporation as a person also poses big problems. In practical effect, the court identifies a corporation as its CEO and board of directors, for they alone will direct the corporation's now virtually unlimited political donations. As any stockholder can attest, no corporation makes the slightest attempt to determine its owners' political opinions. Nonetheless, the Supreme Court has given corporate managers the right to spend unconsulted owners' money to promote their private political interests. It's closer to farce than serious judicial reasoning.

While honoring their dubious legal fictions, the five "strict constructionists" continually demonstrate unprecedented contempt for the well founded legal doctrine of *stare decisis* ("to stand by things decided"). Despite his personal opposition to the death penalty, former Justice John Paul Stevens once deferred to *stare decisis* by voting to uphold a death sentence.

But Chief Justice Roberts lacks Justice Stevens's principle. At his 2005 confirmation hearing, Roberts testified, "It is a jolt to the legal system when you overrule a precedent." Yet in *Citizens United*, Roberts overrode not one precedent, but seven Supreme Court precedents, extending over 103 years of history.

Citizens United is more than a jolt to the legal system; it portends an inexorable degradation of our already money-corrupted political system. It will undoubtedly accelerate our transition from a democratic republic into a full-fledged plutocracy, ruled by an alliance of venal politicians and rich socialists like the hoggish bankers, forever gorging themselves at the public trough.

With this single action plunging us back into the 19th century, the Roberts court has demonstrated its zealous affirmation of Ambrose Bierce's century-old definition of polities: the conduct of public affairs for private profit.

The creation of corporate personhood

At the root of the *Citizens United* decision is the Roberts court's vast extension of the 19th-century legal fiction that judicially defined corporations as persons. How did this preposterous legal fiction, transmogrifying corporations into persons, gain traction? Historically, it was an evolutionary process, occurring in incremental stages over two centuries rather than one stupendous leap into the absurd. In 1819, Chief Justice John Marshall reasonably defined a corporation as "an artificial being," legally endowed with "immortality and . . . individuality." Marshall expressed this metaphorically restrained concept following a key court decision nullifying a state's right to amend a corporate charter.

As the basis for this corporation-favoring decision in 1819, the Supreme Court invoked the sanctity of property rights. Because they affect property rights, corporate charters were deemed inviolable contracts, beyond statutory amendment by state legislatures. Throughout most of our history, capitalist ideology has dominated judicial reasoning.

Among the early injustices created by corporate personhood was the vastly different treatment of small debtors compared with big corporate debtors. Poor debtors were often imprisoned for small debts. In 1820, George Riley spent the first of a six-year sentence in a Boston prison for a debt less than $50. A blind Bostonian with a dependent family was jailed for a $6 debt. Large corporate debtors, however, got favorable bankruptcy treatment. All debtors were equal, but some debtors — i.e., the big corporations — were more equal than others. They were accordingly treated more leniently by the courts.

Nearly 70 years later, the Supreme Court stretched Marshall's "immortal, artificial being" into a person entitled to protection under the 1868 Fourteenth Amendment, which forbids states from depriving ". . . any person of life, liberty, or property, without due process of law; nor to deny any person within its jurisdiction the equal protection of the laws." By logical extension, "person" became a "citizen."

At first, the court resisted constant pressure from high-priced corporate lawyers from granting corporations the same rights as individuals. But in 1886, 18 years after the Fourteenth Amendment's enactment, the court buckled under mounting corporate pressure and defined corporations as persons. A constitutional amendment defining the recently freed slaves' civil rights ironically became a means of consolidating corporate power. Corporate personhood destroyed the states' rights to control corporate malfeasance. For so-called adherents of states' rights, invoked by ultraconservatives whenever they oppose an unwanted federal law, reactionary justices' adherence to the doctrine of corporate personhood makes a farce of their pretense as states' rights defenders.

As previously argued, the *Citizens United* decision furthers the process of turning the United States into a virtual plutocracy. If, as democratic theory posits, the electorate was well informed, knowing who was bribing whom and acting on that knowledge, democracy could survive. But the plutocrats have rigged the game so that corporations can bribe legislators without revealing their identity. (Republicans unanimously oppose Democratically sponsored bills to require publication of political donors, thus allowing donors to secretly buy votes.) Note, too, that the justices perpetrating this monstrous revocation of 103 years of judicial precedent call their opponents judicial activists," guilty of "legislating from the bench."

Constitutional Originalism

The *Citizens United* decision sprang from the Scalia-Thomas-championed theory of Constitutional Originalism –– i.e., that the Supreme Court should interpret the Constitution to mean what its authors meant in 1787 when they wrote it. When the newly elected House of Representatives announced its 2011 "educational" program, which comprised reading the Constitution from the House floor, I wondered how it would treat such embarrassing subjects as the counting of slaves as three-fifths of a person. In retrospect, I see that I should have known that "conservatives" would respond as usual when faced when embarrassing problems. They simply ignore them. The message that they were sponsoring a reading of the Constitution was a bald-faced lie. They sponsored a *partial*, not a total reading, which they had implicitly proposed. They simply skipped the embarrassing sections: Article I, Section 2, paragraph 3 and Article III, Section 2, paragraph 3, and Article I, Section 9, paragraph 1, which allowed slave importation until 1808, 21 years after the Constitution was written. Conservatives can't allow their votaries to be confused by the facts.

Originalism gets no support from the principal founders. In a defense of the threatened Constitution, published first in New York newspapers and later called *The Federalist Papers*, Alexander Hamilton, quoted the great British philosopher, David Hume: "To balance a large state . . . whether monarchical or republican, in general laws, is a work of so great difficulty that no human genius, however comprehensive, is able by mere dint of reason and reflection to effect it. The judgements of many must unite in the work; EXPERIENCE must guide their labours. TIME must bring it to perfection. And the FEELING of inconveniences must correct the mistakes which they *inevitably* fall into, in their first trials and experiments."

Hamilton's advocacy of an evolving development of government is fulfilled by the Constitution's amendment process. If, as the Originalists argue, the founders considered their document to be a perfect version for all eternity, then why did they provide for its amendment? Note, too, that the amendment process was exploited in 1791, only three years after the Constitution's ratification. The amendment provision is an explicit admission that the founders considered their work fallible.

Originalism's follies are continually on display. Writing a dissenting opinion for the three-justice minority in a 2010 juvenile criminal case, Justice Thomas denounced the majority decision that reduced a state court's sentencing of a minor to life in prison without possibility of parole. (The offense was a non-capital crime; no one was killed.) With Scalia's concurrence, Thomas argued that the practices in effect in 1791 (when the Bill of Rights was enacted), constituted the proper judicial guide. At that time, seven-year-old kids could receive capital punishment. Commenting on Thomas's dissent, Justice Stevens said, "Justice Thomas would apparently not rule out a death sentence for a $50 theft by a seven-year-old.

Science be damned

Justice Scalia's Originalism prompts some strange proclamations –– notably on scientific evidence. The late 20th-century advent of DNA evidence is a tremendous technological advance in crime detection. Properly utilized, DNA makes previously doubtful convictions virtually certain. But in its refusal to accept DNA, along with its rejection of the Hamilton-propounded Hume thesis of progressively developing government, Originalism denies scientific advances. In a dissent to a Supreme Court decision granting a death-sentenced prisoner's request for DNA testing, Scalia said, "This court has *never* held that the Constitution forbids the execution of a convicted defendant who has had a full and fair trial, but is later able to convince a habeas court that he is actually innocent." Scalia's reference to a "full and fair trial" in this case ignored contrary facts. Seven of nine key witnesses had recanted their original testimony, the foundation for the questionable conviction.

Dating from an earlier time before the court was dominated by reactionary ideologues, Scalia's foregoing opinion was defeated in the earlier case. But his benighted view prevailed later. The five "conservative" justices united in denying an Alaskan prisoner's request for DNA testing that could prove his innocence after a 14-year imprisonment on a probably false verdict of rape.

In the most appalling aspect of this 2009 decision, Chief Justice Roberts agreed with Alaskan prosecutors that a DNA test could definitively determine the prisoner's guilt or innocence. In his ruling opinion, he nonetheless saw "no necessity for a . . . far-reaching constitutional right of access to this type of evidence."

The Supreme Court heard this case (*District Attorney's Office v. Osborne*) after Alaskan prosecutors challenged a federal appellate court order to allow the requested DNA test. The appellate judges sensibly ordered the test to resolve the prisoner's dubious guilty verdict. Osborne agreed to pay for a DNA test of semen retained since commission of 1994 crime. (Retention of the DNA raised this vital question: Why did Alaska retain this evidence if it intended to bar its use?)

Over the past 17 years Cardoza University's DNA-based Project Innocence has won some 300 exonerations of falsely convicted prisoners. In more than 100 cases, guilty, but unconvicted perpetrators were identified for corrective prosecution.

These overturned verdicts have exposed documented instances of prosecutors' racism, corruption, and sheer stupidity. They have also demonstrated the extreme fallibility of eyewitness identification of criminals.

Many prosecutors fight access to DNA evidence, even in the majority of states that allow it. Concern for their damaged reputations often outweighs prosecutors' dedication to justice. In one preposterous case before the Missouri Supreme Court, prosecutors argued that a convict should be executed even if DNA evidence proved his innocence. One justice, Laura Stith, was incredulous when questioning an assistant state attorney general. "Are you suggesting that even if we find Mr. Armine innocent, he should be executed?" "That's correct, your honor," replied the assistant AG.

In the Osborne case, Justice Samuel Alito buttressed Roberts's opinion with a warning that court orders for DNA testing could induce prisoners "to play games with the system," drowning state courts in a flood of testing demands. States would incur significant unnecessary costs, argued Alito, in a typical conservative exploitation of the slippery-slope fallacy.

In another irrelevant comment, Justice Alito appeared to contradict Roberts's admission that in this case DNA testing would definitively determine a just verdict. Alito claimed that even the most sophisticated DNA testing "often fails to provide absolute proof of anything."

In the four dissenting justices' rebuttal, John Paul Stevens denounced Alaska for refusing all DNA testing requests. He attacked the majority decision with this sensible conclusion: "There is no reason to deny access to the evidence, and there are many reasons to provide it."

In this outrageous denial of common sense, the five "conservative" justices rejected constitutional principles of due process, the demands of simple justice, and a soundly reasoned appellate court decision. They decided that finality in the judicial process trumped truth and justice. The word for these troglodytes is not *conservative*; it is *primitive*.

The founding Originalist

The most notorious Originalist was the late Judge Robert Bork, President Reagan's Supreme Court nominee, whose 1987 Senate rejection is still denounced a quarter century later as the most monstrous legislative injustice ever perpetrated. Apart from his known antipathy to the 1973 abortion-legalizing *Roe v. Wade* decision, Judge Bork was notorious for his opposition to the 1965 *Griswold v. Connecticut* decision, which struck down an archaic statute banning dissemination of birth control information even to married couples. According to Bork, the Supreme Court's discovery that the right to privacy was violated by the Connecticut statute was a heinous violation of the Constitution, which allegedly contains no right to privacy. Bork took great pride in defending the *Griswold* statute regulating sexual behavior as no different from the government's right to enact smoke-abatement ordinances and to generally regulate actions endangering public health. In his refusal to find a right to privacy anywhere in the Constitution, Bork satisfied the primitive yearnings of fundamentalist Christian Republicans, for whom government regulation of the most intimate aspects of life (and death) is a transcendent goal.

Contempt for the founders

When the Originalist zealots don't like the founders' views, they have no problem in ignoring them. They demonstrated this proclivity in their landmark 2008 District of *Columbia v. Heller* decision, in which they ruled (5-4) that the Second Amendment guarantees an individual rather than a collective right to keep and bear arms. *Heller* reversed a landmark 1939 decision, *United States v. Miller*, which established the Second Amendment as a collective, not an individual right.

For nearly 70 years, the *Miller* decision prevailed as the constitutional basis for federal, state, and local gun-control laws. It reversed a lower court decision striking down the 1934 National Firearms Act, which regulated the sale of sawed-off shotguns (popular among criminal gangs). According to the lower court, the firearms act violated an alleged Second-Amendment guarantee for individuals to keep and bear arms, which were regulated by the firearms act.

By unmistakable implication, the 1939 *Miller* decision established the constitutional basis for determining the right to bear arms. To qualify as a firearm under constitutional guarantee, a weapon must satisfy the court's requirement that its ownership have ". . . some reasonable relationship to the preservation or efficiency of a well regulated militia."

In his majority *Heller* opinion, Justice Scalia denied *Miller's* obvious implication. According to Scalia, *Miller* means ". . . only that the Second Amendment does not protect those weapons not typically possessed by law-abiding citizens for lawful purposes, such as short-barrel shotguns." In rebuttal, dissenting Justice Stevens denounced Scalia's opinion as lacking ". . . respect for the well settled views of our predecessors."

At best, Scalia's opinion insults the nation's founders. If the Second Amendment's opening phrase is meaningless, as Scalia implicitly suggests, then the founders were absent-mindedly negligent in drafting the Second Amendment. If the militia contingency is meaningless, why did the founders include it?

Scalia ignores the Second Amendment's historical context. The founders feared a standing army, which they associated with monarchical tyranny. That phobia was expressed in the Declaration of Independence among the grievances against King George III: "He has kept among us in time of peace, Standing Armies without the consent of our legislatures." The founders accordingly placed their trust for national defense in a militia comprising ordinary citizens. This militia obviously required a right to keep and bear arms to qualify it as a fighting force. So if the Second Amendment referred merely to an individual's right to bear arms for self defense, why did the founders confuse the issue by making this right contingent on a well regulated militia? Scalia had no answer.

Conservative ethics

In a landmark decision concerning a state supreme court's chief justice's refusal to recuse himself from a case in which he had a gigantic conflict of interest, the four reactionary justices — Roberts, Alito, Scalia, and Thomas — displayed their low ethical standards. Writing for the majority, Justice Anthony Kennedy, who usually sides with the conservative justices, argued that elected judges who receive huge sums from donors favoring their election must recuse themselves from cases involving these donors. This particular case concerned a $50-million liability judgment against a West Virginia coal company whose president had contributed $3 million to the state Supreme Court Justice Brent Benjamin. Justice Benjamin twice cast the deciding vote to throw out the jury's $50-million liability verdict against his big campaign supporter, Massey Energy. (This large coal company has been perennially guilty of mine-safety violations, including a recent mine disaster in which 29 miners were killed. The plaintiff in *Capputin v. Massey* persuaded the jury that Massey had destroyed its business through fraud.)

Despite this gigantic conflict of interest, the four ultraconservative Supreme Court justices concluded that $3 million was not enough to influence Justice Benjamin's decision in his donor's favor. Justice Benjamin had, after all, assured everyone that his vote was unaffected by the $3-million contribution.

For Justice Benjamin's most adamant defenders, Supreme Court Justices Scalia and Thomas, their sympathy is consistent with their own constantly displayed contempt for their conflicts of interest and ethics generally. In January, 2011, Justice Thomas acknowledged his omission of a legally required financial disclosure statement over the past six years. Common Cause reported Thomas's wife's Heritage Foundation payments of nearly $700,000, 2003 to 2007. That a Supreme Court Justice, presumably versed in the law, could inadvertently "overlook" such a vitally important legal requirement, contained in the 1978 Ethics in Government Act stretches credulity beyond its breaking strain.

Together with his ideological partner, Scalia, Thomas makes no secret of his political extremism. Both justices spoke at a meeting sponsored by Koch Industries, owned by brothers whose father helped to found the idiotic John Birch Society, and in Joe McCarthy fashion, called former President Dwight Eisenhower a Communist. (The Koch brothers haven't retreated from their sire's hyper extremism.)

For his part, Scalia displayed his contempt for judicial ethics by refusing to recuse himself from a case involving his friend, former Vice President Dick Cheney's secret meeting with oil-industry executives. Whereas other justices regularly recuse themselves in similar cases involving conflicts of interest, Scalia said his friendship with Cheney posed no conflict. About the evidence of the friendship, Scalia's invitation to a Cheney-sponsored duck-shooting party, Scalia noted that he didn't share the same shooting quarters! And, of course, only a raving psychopath could suspect that Scalia's vote shielding his friend Cheney's secrecy was influenced in the slightest by their friendship.

As the court's foremost Originalist, Scalia betrays colossal ignorance of the founders' views on judicial ethics. Contrary to the views of founders Madison and Hamilton, the Supreme Court arrogates to itself the right of each justice to decide whether a particular conflict of interest should prompt his recusal from a case. This view collides head-on against Madison's and Hamilton's view. Said Madison, "No man is allowed to be a judge in his own cause, because his interest would certainly bias his judgment and, not improbably, corrupt his integrity," Hamilton was equally adamant: "No man ought certainly to be a judge in his own cause, or in any cause to which he has the least interest or bias."

Justice Scalia refused to recuse himself from another case with an obvious conflict of interest. This case involved a charge of gender bias at Walmart. Scalia's son is co-chairman of Walmart's law firm's labor and employment practice office.

In another affront to judicial ethics, this one concerning religion, Scalia has publicly urged Catholic officeholders to resign if their positions require them to uphold policies contradicting Catholic doctrine. As merely one egregious example, such policies could involve dissemination of information on birth control for welfare recipients. Does anyone who overtly declares his highest allegiance to his religious doctrines rather than United States law belong on the Supreme Court?

The reactionary justices' religious bias was emphatically displayed in the notorious Hobby Lobby case, decided in June, 2014, via another 5-4 decision. It gave privately held corporations the right to deny female employees' access to certain contraceptive methods erroneously believed by Hobby Lobby's owners to induce abortions. In his majority opinion, Justice Samuel Alito found that the health reform contraceptive requirement put a "substantial burden" on religious corporate owners, somehow restricting their religious freedom. The only religious freedom involved in the case was the corporate owners' freedom to impose their morality on their female employees. Nothing prevented the owners from practicing their beliefs or arguing against contraceptives they don't like. The five male justices were asserting their political beliefs, not judicial principles.

Southern racists who opposed blacks' civil rights legislation during the 1960s flaunted bumper stickers reading, "Impeach Earl Warren" (Chief Justice at that time). With greater justification, liberals could flaunt their own impeachment demands, "Impeach Roberts, Alito, Scalia, and Thomas."

CHAPTER 10

Supply-side economics: triumphant myth

"God Almighty in his most holy and wise providence hath so disposed of the condition of mankind, as in all times some must be rich, some poor, some high and eminent in power and dignity, others mean and in submission."

John Winthrop
1630

Ever since the Reagan administration introduced Supply-Side economic ideology as its guiding philosophy in 1981, this intellectually barren concept has dominated U.S. economic policy. There was a partial, and productive, respite during the Clinton administration, when economic growth exceeded growth under the prior Bush administration by at least 60 percent and federal debt was reduced by 16 percent of GDP, compared with Bush's 40 percent increase.

Clinton's uniquely successful economy is merely one proof of Democratic superiority administering the economy over the past 80 years. As discussed in greater detail in Chapter 7, the U.S. economy performed better under Democrats in every basic performance index -- stock-market profits, growth, employment, and debt control. Since 1925, under Democratic Presidents, stock-market S & P values have increased at more than double the rate (13 vs. 6 percent) than under Republican Presidents; GDP per-capita growth has averaged 70 percent higher under Democrats; employment has grown at a similarly higher rate; and federal debt has grown at a similarly lower rate than under Republicans, who never acknowledge these macroeconomic facts when they praise Supply-Side economics.

Two notorious charlatans were the primary sources of Supply-Side ideology. Arthur Laffer originated the Laffer curve, an alleged proof that tax cuts always increase government revenue. The other charlatan was the late Jude Wanniski, an economic con artist promoted by the Wall Street Journal's editorial page.

I encountered Wanniski's mathematical ignorance first hand. In the early 1980s, I sent him an article demonstrating the positive correlation between budget federal budget deficits and three different interest rates -- on Treasury bonds, mortgages, and corporate bonds. Through linear regression analysis, a standard statistical method for such comparisons, I calculated positive correlations, not perfect but undeniable, between budget deficits and interest rates. As dictated by the Law of Supply and Demand, these regressions all showed higher interest rates accompanying higher budget deficits. (Current low interest rates associated with high budget deficits are anomalous, a consequence of persistent economic pessimism and consequent lenders' caution.)

What my regression analysis demonstrated was simply the validity of the Law of Supply and Demand. If a constant supply of credit is reduced by rising government debt, other factors assumed equal, this reduced supply of credit will raise the price of debt, just as a reduced supply of milk with constant demand will raise its price. Because of constantly rising government debt during the Reagan years, Republicans decided to repeal the supply-demand law and deny that budget deficits raised interest rates. Wanniski zealously preached this sermon.

Confronted with my statistical refutation of this thesis, Wanniski scrawled a one sentence reply: "Dear Mr. Griffin," he wrote. "Sorry, I don't understand your paper. The Laffer curve is about as complex as I get." (Anyone who wishes to see this note can contact me for a copy.) This economic guru admitted that he couldn't understand a simple linear-regression analysis, an elementary statistical technique demonstrating the correlation — positive, negative, or neutral — between two variables.

Wanniski's defense of the Laffer curve was farcical. Reportedly written on the back of an envelope during a dinner conversation, the Laffer curve was a joke. Nobel economist Paul Samuelson demolished the Laffer curve in his best-selling text book. An elementary acquaintance with arithmetic reveals the folly. If you halve the tax rate on the capital gains rate, you must double the quantity of the taxed gains to provide equal revenue. And the perpetrators of this rubbish are the deep thinkers of Republican economic philosophy!

Wanniski's problems with economic principles and mathematics only begin with his ignorance of basic statistics; he was also weak on simple fractions. Praising Reagan's tax cuts, Wanniski once wrote, "The economy is one-third bigger now [1991] because of the Reagan reforms and everyone is better off than *if the economy were one-third smaller* [emphasis added]."

The nonsense packed into this 23-word sentence is astonishing. Despite the incontrovertible fact that economic growth under President Carter exceeded Reagan's anemic 2.82-percent average growth rate, Wanniski claims that, without Reagan, GDP would have recorded zero growth throughout Reagan's eight-year tenure. He then compounds the nonsense of this preposterous assertion with a simple arithmetical error. If, as Wanniski postulates, "the economy were one-third smaller" after growing by one-third, it would have experienced an 11-percent decline from its original value. For if GDP grew by one third, to 4/3 of its original volume, and then declined by one-third, the later GDP would be 4/3 x 2/3 = 8/9, or 1/9 less than the original GDP. It would not, as claimed by Wanniski, have been equal to its original value.

Demand-side Economics

Despite its demonstrable failure, Supply-Side economic ideology thrives because of the overwhelming propaganda financed by the Koch Brothers, the American Bankers Association, the Chamber of Commerce and their captive Republican politicians, whose votes are bought through huge campaign contributions. In the three decades dominated by Supply-Side ideology, U.S. economic growth has slowed dramatically while income and wealth distribution has widened back to 1928 levels, in a decade when rampant economic corruption culminated in the 1930s' Great Depression. From a peak of 24 percent of all wages in 1928, earnings of the top one percent fell steadily for the next half century, to a low of 9 percent in 1976, a drastic 62-percent decline. Since then, the top one percent have regained all their lost ground, a 167-percent gain, 24 percent of all wages, in 2007. In this same time span the share of the top .01 percent (i.e., one in 10,000) multiplied more spectacularly, to an average annual $24 million.

Given their initial impetus during the Reagan Administration in the 1980s, tax cuts for the rich, deregulation, privatization, and reduced infrastructure spending have reversed the great growth of the 35 postwar years when average GDP growth was 3.2 percent, at least 25 percent higher than the rate since Reagan took office. Whereas workers formerly shared in the increased productivity, receiving 84 percent of productivity gains in 1947-1979, they have been cut off since then, receiving only 10 percent of the 80-percent productivity gains since 1980. The economy was producing a slightly higher GDP in 2011 than in 2007, but with at least 5 million fewer workers. That's another index of worker exploitation.

Here's the most mindboggling statistic of this period. Since the 1970s, the last decade in which middle-class families thrived economically, the financial industry has increased its share of corporate profits by 300 percent, from 10 percent of all corporate profits during our most prosperous years to 40 percent in 2007. All the other industries — manufacturing, construction, medical, mining, agriculture, retailing, etc. — totaled only 50 percent more than the financial industry's profits. Before the financial industry's absurd growth, the non-financial industries received 90 percent of corporate profits.

Adam Smith be damned

It is seldom recognized how the Republican Party violates the principles promulgated in Adam Smith's classic work, *An Inquiry into the Nature and Causes of the Wealth of Nations*. Smith was to economics what Isaac Newton was to physics, the pioneering founder of his science. Republicans profess to follow Smith's policies, but it's doubtful that any of them have plowed through *The Wealth of Nations*. Far from the Republican apotheosis of capitalists, Smith held them in contempt. His sentiments about capitalists resembled Karl Marx's. Here's a sample:

"The interest of the dealers . . . in any particular branch of trade or manufacturers in always in some respects different from, and even opposite to that of the public. To widen the market and to narrow the competition, is always the interest of the dealers. To widen the market may frequently be agreeable to the interest of the public, but to narrow the competition must always be against it, and can only enable the dealers, by raising their profits above what they would naturally be, to levy, for their own benefit, an absurd tax upon the rest of their fellow citizens. The proposal of any new law or regulation of commerce which comes from this order, ought always to be listened to with great precautions, and ought never to be adopted till after having been long and carefully examined, . . . with the most suspicious attention. It comes from an order of men . . . who have generally an interest to deceive and even to oppress the public, and who accordingly have, upon many occasions, both deceived and oppressed it.

Smith's views on taxing the rich would not only ban him from the Republican Party; they would open him to the "class-warfare" charge leveled at President Obama. "It is not very unreasonable that the rich should contribute to the public expense, not only in proportion to their revenue, but something more than that proportion," said Smith. That's a clear advocacy for the progressive income tax and a condemnation for the flat tax overwhelmingly favored by Republicans. Smith also opposed vast differences in wealth distribution. He approved another economist's proposal, "To remedy inequality of riches as much as possible, by relieving the poor and burdening the rich." These statements make clear how Smith would react to the Republicans' efforts to reduce taxes on the rich and increase them on the poor at a time when the rich pay the lowest proportionate taxes in nearly a century.

On the Republicans' perennial demand for less regulation of corporations, Smith again denounced extreme laissez-faire economic philosophy. Banks, in particular, require tight regulation, according to Smith:

"Though the principles of the banking trade may appear somewhat abstruse, the practice is capable of being reduced to strict rules. To depart upon any occasion from these rules, in consequence of some flattering speculation of extraordinary gain, is almost always extremely dangerous and frequently fatal to the banking company which attempts it."

The above passage from *The Wealth of Nations*, written nearly 240 years ago, seems a preternaturally accurate prophecy of the 2008 financial meltdown resulting from the banks' reckless indulgence in "speculation of extraordinary gain," unrestrained by the "strict rules" advocated by Smith. If Smith's regulatory principles ("strict rules" for banks), had been followed during the Bush 43 Administration, there would have been no subprime mortgage fiasco and no financial meltdown. Against the efforts even of Republican state governors concerned about reckless mortgage-lending, the Bush Administration rejected the conservatives' normal promotion of states' rights. It passively approved mortgage-lending policies characterized by a reckless drive to maximize profits regardless of risk. Countrywide, a major lender, instructed its agents never to reject a borrower regardless of his obvious inability to pay. Mortgages of $700,000 were extended to borrowers with $17,000 incomes. Applicants were encouraged to lie about their incomes. Appraisers dishonestly issued bloated property appraisals. Credit-rating agencies, operating with blatant conflicts of interest still unresolved, issued AAA rating on junk bonds comprising largely worthless mortgages. The entire real-estate industry was complicit in this inexcusable fiasco. And the Republican Party, bribed by overwhelming political contributions from bankers and their associates, still refuses to acknowledge the obvious source of the meltdown, which it attributes to excessive government regulation.

For the 18th-century precursors of the 21st-century Republicans protesting regulation as an unwarranted infringement of liberty, Smith had a cogent rebuttal:

"Such regulation may, no doubt, be considered . . . a violation of natural liberty. But these exertions of the natural liberty of a few individuals, which might endanger the security of the whole society are, and ought to be, restrained by a . . . all governments . . . The obligation of building party walls, in order to prevent the communication of fire, is a violation of our natural liberty, exactly of the same kind with the regulation of the banking trade which are proposed here."

Free market or free lunch?

The most convincing way to rebut Supply-Side economics is, of course, to demonstrate how it has failed to fulfill its predictions. In the past, low tax rates on the rich have been correlated with low growth, low employment, rising federal debt, and low stock-market profits, all spectacularly displayed during the younger Bush's administration. Even more spectacular is the lack of correlation between CEO performance and pay. This pay-for-performance principle is constantly parroted by Sean Hannity, Rush Limbaugh, and other propaganda hacks preaching Horatio Alger mythology to the masses. Oil-driller Nabors Industries' stock has trailed the S & P average for over a decade, and in November, 2011, was down 20 percent. Yet Nabors paid CEO Eugene Isenberg $100 million to give up the presidency (while remaining as board chairman). Gannett's departing CEO got a $37-million severance package after presiding over a catastrophic 87 percent stock decline in his six-year tenure. In another late 2011 instance, Hewlett Packard's CEO, fired after a 46 percent drop in his company's stock price, floated to earth in an effulgent $13-million golden parachute. Far from the exception, these outlandish rewards for failure have almost become the rule. Crony capitalists serving on boards of directors routinely reverse their loyalty from betrayed shareholders to company executives.

Proof that the system works this way is contained in the statistics for the year 2000. Despite a 12-percent decline in the stock indexes, executive pay rose 22 percent. In other words, there was a negative correlation between the pay-for-performance principle preached by free marketers and the actual statistics. (If CEO pay had declined as decreed by free-market ideology, average CEO pay would have been 28 percent less than it was.) In successful years, of course, executive pay rises even more spectacularly than it does in losing years, demonstrating the total irrelevance between pay and performance.

There's still another way to view this phenomenon. In the last three decades, American CEOs' pay has increased 10 times as fast as workers' pay. Whereas CEOs formerly averaged 40 times times workers' pay, they now average about 400 times workers' pay. In the past 30 years, stocks' performance and GDP, two basic indexes of economic health, have declined from the previously 30 years. Confronted with these damning facts, how can anyone seriously argue that U.S. executives' competence has increased spectacularly in the past 30 years?

Questions like this get no comment from Republican propagandists. They simply assume, as a self-evident proposition, that executives are generally paid in accordance with their economic worth, a truism so obvious that there is no need to defend such a patently obvious axiom. House Speaker John Boehner dismisses calls for tax increases on the rich as socialistic policies aimed at "job-creating" entrepreneurs. They are indeed job creators in countries like India, China, and Mexico. Multinational corporations have added 2.9 million foreign jobs over the past decade. For the U.S., however, they are job destroyers, having cut 2.4 million American jobs in the same decade, according to the Center on Budget and Priorities. Outsourcing American jobs has vastly increased corporate profits and pay of corporate executives and hedge-fund manufacturers.

These job-creation myths are possible only through the remarkable success of politically reactionary propaganda in convincing mass minds to ignore the facts. Confronted with facts contradicting their propaganda, they simply ignore them. Boehner doesn't deny the truth of the job-outsourcing facts. He simply refuses to acknowledge them. On job creation, Republicans have largely succeeded in obliterating rational public debate, which they have reduced to a contest of slogans hammered into receptively naive brains.

Wanniski v. Keynes

Supply-side economics is the ideological antithesis of Keynesian economics. Keynes considered demand as the dominant variable in the demand-supply relationship. Supply-siders counter with this argument: If you can somehow increase supply, you thereby promote demand. Accordingly, every economic action should be subordinated to the interest of increasing supply. Lower taxes, low employee wages, and less government regulation all contribute to increasing supply, the paramount goal. Increase supply, and by some ineffable magic demand will spring up, consumption will increase, and the economy will expand.

This philosophy is contradicted by the economy's performance, Keynesian theory, and by common sense. Though they overwhelmingly back Republicans with their political donations, businessmen contradict Republican Supply-side doctrine with their comments on the stagnant economy of 2011. "Business demand is what drives hiring," says a quoted businessman, repeating what most businessmen say about the stalled economy. They are implicitly contradicting Supply-side economic theory. Widespread unemployment most obviously reduces consumer demand, a truism implicitly denied by Supply-side Republicans. They also implicitly deny that consumers account for nearly 70 percent of the nation's economic activity.

Reduced to its mathematical relations, the Law of Supply and Demand demonstrates the primacy of demand over supply as the more important, independent variable. You can readily imagine a situation in which there is no demand for a given supply –– for example, 20-foot-long golf clubs. But free-market theory decrees that demand always produces supply. It is a basic economic tenet that businessmen will attempt to satisfy any demand that promises profits. Equilibrium between supply and demand balances out at a price dependent upon the intensity of demand and the quantity of supply. Supply-side theory is thus contradicted by the basic premise of free-market theory, that demand for anything will always stimulate its supply.

Supply-siders always justify their theory with the argument that the so-called free market justifies the apportionment of corporate profits, which, as previously noted, have become ridiculously high for bankers, hedge-fund managers, and other members of the financial industry. To demonstrate the folly of this viewpoint, consider a thought experiment, a device often used by scientists to illustrate a principle. What would happen if the nation's lobbyists, recipients of huge pay from corporations, dropped dead overnight? Compare this consequence with what would happen if the nation's surgeons suddenly dropped dead. The surgeons' deaths would obviously deal a catastrophic blow to our society. But if every lobbyist dropped dead, the economy would experience a huge benefit at the removal of these obstructive parasites.

How to succeed through secrecy

The propagandists who preach the glories of Supply-side economics and denounce the debilitating horror of government programs betray their faith in their hypertrophied hypocrisy. Senate Minority Leader Mitch McConnell constantly rails against government projects in general and clean-energy projects in particular. But these persistent protests didn't stop him from personally appealing to Energy Secretary Steven Chu to approve $235 million in federal loans for an electric-vehicle plant in Franklin, Kentucky. This project would create 4,000 jobs, claimed McConnell, who almost daily denounces failed job-creation efforts. McConnell's support for the project followed the efforts of a Kentucky-based lobbyist, Robert Babbage, a big contributor to McConnell's electoral campaigns. (Despite his opposition to socialistic policies, McConnell also supported accelerated depreciation for Kentucky racehorse owners; socialism for the rich is OK by Republican standards.) Other Republican congressmen –– Rep. Lamar Smith of Texas, Fred Upton of Michigan, Cliff Stearns of Florida, and Paul Ryan of Wisconsin –– all sought federal loan guarantees or grants for clean-energy projects in their states. It's all kept secret from Tea Party supporters. Fox News, Sean Hannity, and Rush Limbaugh will never tell how these hypocrites inflame their simple-minded votaries with fiery anti-government sermons while secretly seeking socialistic subsidies for their contributors.

Tea Partiers' ignorance about their "conservative" congressmen is paralleled by their ignorance about their own dependence on government programs. This is a general failure, applying to liberals and conservatives alike. Asked if they ever "used a government social program," 59 percent of Americans denied that they had ever used even one. Questioned in further detail about their use of 21 different federal programs –– Social Security, unemployment insurance, student loans, home-mortgage tax deductions, etc. –– only 6 percent denied that they had ever benefited from a federal program. Carrying their investigation further, to discover if there were differences between liberals and conservatives in their general ignorance, the Cornell Survey Research Institute found that "extremely conservative" respondents were considerably more ignorant than their "extremely liberal" counterparts, who were 20 percent more likely to acknowledge personal use of a government program. The angry old Tea Party man, who furiously told his congressman to "keep your government hands off my Medicare," was no anomaly.

Ignorance of their dependence on government programs accompanies the abysmal mass ignorance of economic theory, especially among conservatives. Keynes recognized the boom-bust cycles afflicting free-market capitalism. (Between 1870 and 1910, the United States experienced a series of panics and depressions lasting up to five years (1873-1878, 1893-1898). To alleviate the hardship attending these alternating panics and booms, Keynes proposed government stimulus in times of slack demand offset, balanced with higher taxes and reduced government spending in times of price-raising high demand.

President Obama follows Keynes with his proposal for infrastructure spending, repairing or replacing the nation's huge backlog of deteriorating schools, highways, bridges, mass-transit systems, dams, water and sewage-treatment plants, many over a half-century old and decrepitly polluting our waterways. This longterm neglect now carries a $2-trillion price tag, according to the American Society of Civil Engineers. We could simultaneously upgrade the nation's economic performance through expanded, federally aided infrastructure maintenance and replacement, put several million unemployed construction workers to work, while stimulating demand via their wages. Moreover, the current economic environment is an especially propitious time for launching public works projects. Costs would be low because of low interest rates, workers' pay, and materials' costs, all depressed by low demand in the stagnant economy. Waiting for boom times drastically raises construction costs.

Supply-siders, however, say no to these obvious arguments. Fiscal responsibility, never mentioned during the Bush era when

Dick Cheney famously said, "Reagan proved that deficits don't matter," is now the only economic factor that does matter. Not only infrastructure construction, but teacher hiring, restoring some of the recession's half million public workers' job losses and improving our faltering educational system, don't merit consideration compared with the job-creating benefits of shielding billionaires from even a one percent tax increase.

The unique selling proposition

What accounts for the immense success of Republican propaganda –– notably, the Murdoch TV and talk-radio racket –– in duping masses of Americans is the application of scientific mass advertising methods in politics. A half century ago, Rosser Reeves, a highly successful advertising executive, introduced what he call "the unique selling proposition (USP). It was a technique for hammering home simple thoughts into simple minds, focused on the idea of stressing single, simple theses, not confusing consumers with complexity. (Reeves could have learned this lesson from Adolph Hitler, who, in *Mein Kampf,* revealed his technique for duping the masses: ". . . the most brilliant propagandist technique will yield no success unless one fundamental principle is borne in mind constantly and with unflagging attention. It must confine itself to a few points and repeat them over and over.")

Republican politicians and propagandists have learned this lesson. As the previous discussion has demonstrated, the Republican Party has honed its economic message into the simplest imaginable formula: Tax cuts for the rich promote economic growth and job creation. Constant repetition drives this simple message into simple minds. Historically, the market grew at a 25-percent faster rate when the top tax rate ranged from 70 to 80 percent than when it was 35 percent or less. But by sedulously preventing the public from being confused by easily verified statistical facts, constant repetition of this lie enabled Republicans to dupe a large segment of the public into believing their unique selling proposition.

Fighting back

Britain's reaction to Rupert Murdoch's midsummer 2011 cellphone-hacking scandal contains a lesson in how to free ourselves from the grip of deceptive propaganda. As Carl Bernstein points out, Murdoch corrupted three vitally important British institutions: the political system, the media, and even the police. Murdoch's journalistic thugs routinely bribed Scotland Yard police for information needed for cellphone hacking. So avaricious for sensational news was Murdoch's now defunct scandal sheet, *News of the World*, that its journalists planted messages on a murdered girl's cellphone that gave her parents false hope that she was still alive, though Murdoch's minions knew she was dead. Britain's previously apathetic public exploded in mass fury at this damning revelation. And the British Parliament appeared ready to challenge Murdoch's son's testimony that, despite his status as CEO of *News of the World*, he knew nothing about the newspaper's rampant practice of phone hacking to get salacious and other sensational stories.

The United States has good reason to follow Britain's lead in repudiating Murdoch. Aided by politicians like former Senate Majority Leader Trent Lott (R, MS), whose votes he bought with huge political contributions, Murdoch extended his publishing empire in the U.S. No British-style revulsion with Murdoch has hit America; Fox News rolls on, sedulously preaching its "fair-and-balanced" Republican propaganda. But there are signs that the public is fed up with extremist propaganda. Disapproval of the Tea Party has doubled since the outrageous congressional debt-crisis politicking by Tea-Party congressmen brought the federal government perilously close to default and precipitated big stock-market losses. The pathetic performance of Texas Governor Perry in Presidential debates significantly reduce voters' enthusiasm for this simple-minded charlatan. Michele Bachmann's recklessly irresponsible warning that the HPV vaccine can cause mental retardation seems to have alienated the public. From President Obama's ridicule of the preposterous "class warfare" charge, we can conclude that he finally accepts the nature of politics as a contact sport.

A notorious example of socialism for the rich occurred in the 1990s, when a proposal to finance the U.S. Coast Guard with user charges from yacht owners, major beneficiaries of the Coast Guard's safety program. The big yacht owners, some of whom spend $20 million annually to staff their crews, killed that idea by screaming to their congressmen. General taxpayers, who get no benefit from the Coast Guard, nonetheless continue to subsidize it for billionaire yacht owners. And there is plenty of conservative support for millionaires' farm subsidies received by Michelle Bachmann and Rick Perry.

Hitler's unheeded lesson

One explanation for extremists' astonishing success in politics despite their minority status is the inability of emotionally balanced, reasonable people to believe that fanatics arc really serious. A spectacular historical instance concerns the refusal of 1930s' world leaders to believe that Adolph Hitler meant what he said in *Mein Kampf,* when he referred to the missed opportunity of gassing 15,000 Jews at the beginning of World War I. According to Hitler's tortured reasoning, the gassing of these Jews could have some saved a million German lives lost at the front. This passage occurred very late in Hitler's tedious tome. But someone in the West might have noted it as a harbinger of the Holocaust. World leaders maintained their naive skepticism even after Hitler gained power and committed preliminary acts pointing directly to the Holocaust. A similar incredulity, even less excusable, evidently afflicts the mainstream press and Democratic Party officials who cling to the forlorn hope that congressional Republicans really didn't mean it when they signed Grover Norquist's pledge never, ever to raise taxes on the rich.

It's a sign of the stupefied times when bank executives, the same people whose reckless policies created the subprime mortgage fiasco and the ensuing financial meltdown, warn against regulation designed to thwart future meltdowns because such regulation would curtail financial innovation. There couldn't be a better reason to enact and enforce regulations that discourage "financial innovation." Innovations —— notably, collateralized debt obligations —— caused the 2008 financial meltdown.

CHAPTER 11

The Plutocratic Populists

"The rights and interests of the working men will be protected . . . not by the labor agitators, but, by the Christian men to whom God, in his infinite wisdom, has given control of the property interests of the country."

George F. Bair,
19th-century
coal-mine owner

In 2014, despite diminished public support for the Tea Party, that benighted group nonetheless shows how deep the dumbing of America has progressed in the early 21st century. A recent poll result, naturally from the racist Bible Belt, should resolve any doubt that the Republican Party —— notably Tea Party extremists —— embraces a grossly disproportionate share of the nation's imbeciles. Assigning blame for the negligent federal response to Hurricane Katrina, more Louisiana Republicans cited President Obama than cited George W. Bush. By a slim margin (29 to 28 percent), these Obama-blaming morons assigned presidential responsibility to Obama four years before he was inaugurated.

Further evidence of Tea Party ignorance comes from a Sixty-Minutes report on Kentucky's fake Social-Security disability claims. A state-indulged system of corrupt claims, promoted by prostitute lawyers and medical doctors, gives Kentuckians three times their proportional share of disability claims. These costs threaten the system's survival. Yet the ignorant state Tea Partiers continually howl about needless federal spending, totally oblivious of their state's outsized role in wasteful federal spending.

In the 2012 Republican presidential primary in the Tea Party's core state, South Carolina, candidate Newt Gingrich, showed how to exploit the fanatics' fury. Excoriating the hapless CNN moderator, John King, for raising the question of his infidelity, Gingrich blamed King for perpetuating mainstream media bias. To this charge, the Republican audience responded with a fury matching Gingrich's. Television viewers described how they exultantly leaped from their chairs at Gingrich's denunciation of King and his media colleagues. Polls showed large, immediate gains for Gingrich: he triumphed with a decisive 14-point margin over previously favored Milt Romney, who suffered a dramatic, if temporary loss.

Stupidity and Immorality

"Its recent actions demonstrate that the Tea Party's intellectual vacuum is accompanied by an equally appalling moral vacuum. Representative Scott DesJarlais (R, TN) won his 2014 primary despite his stupefyingly gross hypocrisy. A medical doctor, Representative Des Jarlais was fined by his state's board of medical examiners for carrying on sexual affairs with patients. Equally horrific was his approval of his wife's abortions. This despite his fanatical support of the Republican anti-abortion doctrine, to deny abortions even to rape victims."

Rick Santorum posed a different moral problem than DesJarlais, but he, too, demonstrated the dual problem of intellectual and moral defects. Like his fellow Republican candidates, Santorum repeatedly lied about President Obama's statements, repeating these lies even after correction. But his chief problem involves his medieval obsession with sex and his incredibly bizarre beliefs. Nearly a half century ago, in the landmark 1965 Griswold v. Connecticut Supreme Court case, an archaic state law banning dissemination of birth-control information was ruled unconstitutional. It was, said the court, an infringement of constitutional privacy rights. Santorum opposes that decision, arguing that states should have the right to ban contraception. He is not content to prescribe his own morality and follow it. Like medieval Catholic theologians, he must obtrude his morality on others. Santorum espouses a moral dictatorship of the busybodies.

Associated with his medieval morality, some bizarre opinions mark Santorum's political philosophy. As one notorious example, he blames the Catholic pedophilia scandal on "academic, political, and cultural liberalism in America." This is truly astonishing. Santorum absolves ostensively incorruptible conservatives from their vicious betrayal of sheep presumably protected by conservative shepherds. Instead he blames liberals for conservatives' corruption.

To see how strange Santorum's opinion is we must review the pedophile scandal. The Catholic hierarchy was guilty of an outrageous sequence of morally corrupt acts, notably:

- intimidation of molested altar boys' parents, demanding that they keep quiet
- transfer of known pedophile priests to other, unwarned parishes, where they continued their depredations
- failure to report pedophile crimes to police
- participation in a Vatican-sanctioned coverup

How can Santorum seriously blame these heinous acts on liberals? Why, if conservatism is such a powerful philosophy, did its presumably most principled practitioners become such abject weaklings that they couldn't resist their opponents' corrupt philosophy? Santorum never attempted to explain.

Equally bizarre is Santorum's twisted views on abortion. Attempting to justify his demand that the federal government, which he claims should be curtailed in its interference in citizens' lives, should nonetheless force rape victims to bear their rapists' babies, Santorum says, "To put rape victims through another trauma of an abortion, I think is too much to ask." For sheer, adamant refusal to consider others' feelings, this statement is hard to beat. For a rapist's victim the trauma is not an abortion, which she almost always favors, but a government-enforced birth. Santorum's failure to admit this inescapable, elementary fact can be attributed only to willful blindness or dishonesty. It is, however, consistent with his sick psychology, manifest in his decision to show his wife's dead fetus to their children.

Lying with impunity

Santorum's lying does not distinguish him from other Republican presidential candidates, but it is strange behavior for someone known for ostentatious displays of public piety. What Tea Party favorites have learned, however, is that they can lie with impunity; Republican extremists will reward them rather than punish them for lying about opponents. On the birth control issue raised in the 2012 winter, Santorum denounced "liberals" who allegedly claim that "only people of nonfaith can come into the public square and make their case." As usual, when extremists make false charges, they never provide evidence to back them up. No one to my knowledge, certainly not President Obama, has ever said that religious people are not free to publicly argue their case. But why allow the facts to confuse your audience when you can inflame your supporters with a plausibly sounding lie?

Lying has become so pervasive for Republican politicians that they have begun to defend it as merely the normal practice of politics, following the Communist Party rule that the ends justify the means. Two instances from the 2012 primary campaign illustrate the process. Before his exposure as a simpleton too stupid to compete even against other intellectually impaired opponents, Texas Governor Rick Perry excoriated President Obama for accusing Americans of being lazy. It was an incontrovertible lie, obvious from reading the full quote from which it was abstracted: "There are a lot of things that make foreigners see the U.S. as a great opportunity. But we've been a little lazy, I think, over the past couple of decades." Perry omitted the first sentence, thereby annihilating the context.

Mitt Romney published a television and containing a similar distortion. It shows Obama saying, "If we keep talking about the economy, we're going to lose." This is an even worse distortion than Governor Perry's. Here's what the President actually said, "Senator McCain's campaign actually said, and I quote, 'If we keep talking about the economy, we're going to lose'" Confronted with this obvious lie, a Romney adviser defended it with an incredibly cynical reply, "It's ludicrous . . . . to say that an ad is taking something out of context. All ads do that. They are manipulative pieces of persuasive art."

Almost as remarkable as the defense of deliberate lying is the cynical claim that all ads dishonestly ignore context. Whatever their defects, most ads do not exploit the deceptive deleting of context. But, of course, the chief problem with the Romney adviser's statement is its blasé defense of lying as a perfectly ethical political tactic. In no previous political era would you encounter such an astonishing defense. But in those earlier days the idea that lying propaganda should be admired purely for its aesthetic quality as "persuasive art" was beyond consideration as a public statement.

What this idea signifies is a truly horrifying thought for those who accept the traditional theory of American democracy, as promulgated by the founders. Democracy, said the founders, can thrive only with an intelligent, informed citizenry. It has always been painfully obvious that the malefactors of wealth have never harbored the slightest compunction against exploiting the masses. But in the past, they at least felt the necessity of obscuring their contempt. Now, however, they see no need to hide this contempt. And the Tea Party faithful have demonstrated that they deserve their exploiters' contempt. Lies, and the evidence that they are lies, have little or no power to enlighten them.

Tea Party, then and now

That the Tea Party exists in an intellectual vacuum has been evident since its ludicrous origin. The 21st-century Tea Party is founded upon a preposterous historical error about its similarity to its 18th-century predecessor. In 1773, the original Tea Party's complaint was, of course, "No taxation without representation." Its protest was directed against the British Parliament, which had previously set the New England colonies aflame with the Stamp Act of 1765. With the ensuing passage of tea taxes, Parliament further inflamed the colonists.

There is not the remotest similarity between the contemporary and the original 1773 Tea Party. In stark contrast with the original Tea Party, which was deprived of political representation in Parliament, contemporary Tea Partiers participated in droves in the 2010 and 2014 congressional elections. With their high voting percentage, they are numerically over-represented in Congress. This anomaly is also perpetrated by the majority of Republican-dominated states' ubiquitous gerrymandering, which gave Republicans control of the 2013 House of Representatives despite their loss of the popular vote by 1.5 million to the Democrats. Their constantly parroted refrain, "to take our country back," is a self-evident absurdity. They assume that they deserve special political consideration, like spoiled children.

Who are the Tea Partiers?

Tea Partiers are disproportionately white, male, old, Christian evangelical, racist, Republican. Nearly two-thirds, three times as many as non-Tea Partiers, get their news from Fox News. That fact explains their general ignorance. As a startling example of their gullibility, nearly two-thirds of Fox News viewers believed that "the U.S. has found clear evidence in Iraq that Saddam Hussein was working closely with the Al Qaeda terrorist organization." Only one-third of non-Fox-News viewers (still far too many) believed that sedulously cultivated lie (chiefly by former Vice President Cheney, who challenged his critics to prove that Saddam Hussein did not conspire with Al Qaeda to provoke the 9/11 attacks. See Chapter 3, "Reversing the Burden of Proof"). And 86 percent doubt global-warming science, nearly twice as many as non-Tea Partiers.

As evidence of their racist proclivities, white Tea Partiers, more than any other political category, believe the following:

- Blacks' problems are generally overemphasized (52 percent)
- Providing benefits for the poor promotes poverty (76 percent)
- Obama was not born in the U.S.
- Obama is moving the nation toward socialism

Tea Partiers are also more likely than other Americans to be NRA fanatics, anti-abortionists, homophobics, and anti-business regulation. Tea-Party membership is 98 percent whites with 1 percent each, blacks and Hispanics. Tea Partiers are also disproportionately represented among evangelical Christians who deny the theory of Evolution. In short, they constitute a society of dunces, the intellectual dregs of American society.

Suckers, Inc.

The most pathetic aspect of the Tea Partiers' confused cause has to be their evident ignorance of their exploiters. Chief among these are the Koch Brothers, whose combined $43 billion wealth ranks them near the world's richest men. Their predecessors created the American Liberty League in 1934, to oppose President Franklin D. Roosevelt's Social Security, Securities Exchange Commission, and anti-labor laws. Today's Koch Brothers back similarly reactionary causes -- repeal of health-care reform, abolition of industry safety regulations, Social Security, Medicaid, and Medicare, unemployment compensation, and programs generally aiding the poor.

It is understandable that the more well-to-do Tea Partiers, the angry old white men who do a little better financially than the average American, would sympathize with denying help to the poor. But their opposition to the Consumer Financial Protection Bureau (CFPB) can only be attributed to ignorance. Over the years, American banks have expanded their sleazy exploitation of customers to extraordinary levels of chiseling, tripling or quadrupling delinquent credit rates over former levels. Industry executives and their Republican lackeys attacked President Obama's first choice for CFPB chief, Elizabeth Warren, and Obama failed to nominate her.

Among Warren's alleged anti-bank crimes was advocating clear, concise credit-card and mortgage contracts. Her industry opponents clearly want to perpetuate the cozy rackets duping the naive and unwary that have proved increasingly profitable in recent years. Like almost everyone else, Tea Partiers would personally benefit from an aggressively active CFPB.

In fighting creation of the CFPB, the bankers' lobby inadvertently highlighted the source of the 2008 financial meltdown. One of the lobbyists' objections to the CFPB is that it might thwart "financial innovation." If the CFPB can thwart financial innovation that alone would justify its creation. Financial innovation produced the 2008 financial meltdown. Without financial innovations like collectivized debt obligations (CDOs), the subprime mortgage fiasco could not have occurred. Before the creation of CDOs, mortgages were retained by their issuers, who remained on the hook if the debtors defaulted. When they retained responsibility for mortgage payments, mortgage bankers were forced to investigate borrowers' credit worthiness. Under these conditions -- i.e., creditors retaining the risk of the debtors' defaults -- there were naturally very few defaults. With creation of CDOs, which bundled thousands of mortgages into bonds sold to pension funds and other investors, the system finally collapsed. Freed from default risks, mortgage brokers exploited opportunities for multiplying their profits exponentially. They issued more low-quality mortgages, passing the default risk onto the purchasers of their CDOs. Countrywide, probably the most corrupt, grew to a hugely bloated size, pursuing an executive-ordered policy of never rejecting an applicant, regardless of obvious inability to repay the loan. Countrywide's brokers encouraged applicants to lie about their financial resources and consequent ability to repay. Credit-rating agencies, currying favor with mortgage issuers whose bonds they rated, gave triple-A ratings to CDOs correctly considered junk. Appraisers falsified their reports to keep the game going with ever higher stakes. As home prices inevitably skyrocketed, climbing 85 percent in constant dollars in the 1996-2006 decade, the game continued until the inevitable defaults shattered the fantastic edifice into an ignominious heap of rubble. By mid-2012, home prices had declined by 40 percent or more below their 2007 peak value.

Another innovation, the credit-default swap was, at bottom, a crooked gambling insurance scheme designed to produce huge profits for hedge funds and other speculating parasites. Credit-default swaps were analogous to insurance contracts taken out on one's neighbor's house. Bailing out the losers in credit default swaps multiplied the housing-bubble losses exponentially. Wall Street had learned nothing from the earlier savings-and-loan fiasco.

Corruption thrived, and is still thriving, in this parasitical financial economy. J.P. Morgan Chase, Goldman Sachs, and other huge financial organizations profited from treachery, betting against clients for whom they had a fiduciary responsibility. They conned their clients with reports praising investments that they knew were doomed to fail.

The real socialists

The most ironically humorous aspect of the bankers' excoriation of Obama's alleged socialism is their enthusiastic support of socialism when they profit from it. Bankers denounced Obama's overhaul of student lending as a "government takeover." They demanded continuation of a socialistic program that paid the banks $8 billion annually to serve as useless middlemen. These bank middlemen ran no risk whatever. When students defaulted, U.S. taxpayers guaranteed their profits. The same bankers who denounced proposals to create government-subsidized construction jobs to repair our deteriorating our deteriorating highways, bridges, dams, sewage and water-supply systems demanded a far less justifiable socialistic policy that required taxpayers to pay roughly $250,000 annually to each subsidized banker middleman for doing no productive work. President Obama appropriately called student-loan reform a no-brainer. The Tea Party's siding with the bankers on this issue demonstrates their hopeless ignorance.

The public generally, and Tea Partiers particularly, mistakenly believe that government aid to the poor constitutes the biggest increases in government spending. This is a gross error. As a proportion of total benefits, aid to the poor has declined by 33 percent since 1980, whereas aid received by the highest 20 percent of earners has increased by 45 percent. There is also gross hypocrisy in the Tea Partiers' and their favored congressmen's pretense that they really favor draconian cuts in federal entitlement programs.

The late, unlamented Republican presidential candidate, Representative Michelle Bachmann, exemplifies Tea Party hypocrisy. Among the least excusable of wasteful federal spending is the $20 billion annually spent on millionaire farmers, who hog 80 percent of the subsidies purportedly justified by its necessity to preserve the "family farm." Michelle Bachmann's family shared in this federal waste, collecting $251,000 between 1995 and 2009. Her claim that this money went to her late father-in-law is contradicted by congressional disclosure forms, which list herself and her husband as financial partners receiving farm income of $103,000. Moreover, Bachmann's husband gets federal aid for his mental-health clinic, which dispenses "Christian counseling." He has collected $137,000 in federal Medicaid payments since 2005. Marcus Bachmann got these subsidies despite his religiously based "reparative therapy," a farcical attempt to "pray away the gay" — i.e., to make gays straight through prayer. Condemned by psychologists as anti-scientific nonsense, this absurd practice springs from the homophobic religious community's belief that homosexuality is a moral choice, not an innate proclivity. It has dangerous consequences for gays duped into attempting it.

Bachmann's hypocrisy as a recipient of federal subsidies that she denounces for everyone else is common among Tea-Party supported congressmen. Information about this hypocrisy is difficult to obtain. Fox News protects Tea Party politicians by suppressing negative news about them, keeping its viewers in blissful ignorance about their political heroes. It took an enterprising *New York Times* reporter to ferret out the news through the Freedom of Information Act. Among the federally financed projects sought by Tea Party congressmen were beach-repair projects, a $700-million bridge construction in Minnesota, and a $300-million harbor-dredging project in Charleston, South Carolina. These projects were defended with the usual denials — that pork for Minnesota, South Carolina, and New Jersey was not the same as pork for other states. For the South Carolina harbor-dredging project, Senator Lindsay Graham had an additional "argument" — a blackmail threat to block President Obama's nominees for judgeships and other posts requiring Senate approval. Commenting on the blackmail's success in assuring federal aid, Representative Tim Scott (R, S.C.) credited persistence with assuring approval of this worthy project. Like the pedophile priests who betrayed their docile flock, these Tea Party hypocrites deserve special contempt beyond that earned by conventional politicians for betraying their self-proclaimed moral superiority in opposing government subsidies.

Ayn Rand dupes the Tea Party

It was probably inevitable that the gullible Tea Party would be duped by the world's most perdurably successful literary con artist, the late Ayn Rand. Tea Partiers fueled the most recent sales surge of Rand's alleged masterpiece, *Atlas Shrugged*, second only to the Bible in total sales over the past half century. Blissfully unaware of Rand's colossal ignorance, Tea-Party leaders praise Rand's economic myths as cogent warnings against government intervention into the free market.

Atlas Shrugged contains an utterly preposterous economic scenario contradicted by subsequent events soon after its 1957 publication. In Rand's scenario, a talented industrialist develops a marvelous new steel alloy whose increased strength could, for example, lengthen railroad and highway bridge spans. This entrepreneur is thwarted in his efforts to introduce the new improved steel by a vicious federal bureaucracy determined at all costs to deny the nation its economic benefits.

Rand's fictional scenario collides head-on against reality. Within five years of *Atlas Shrugged's* publication, the U.S. steel industry introduced not just one, but five new high-strength alloy steels into the American construction industry. Through skillful use of manganese, silicon, nickel, and other alloys, plus the heat-strengthening of one new steel to a yield strength double that of conventional (ASTM A36) structural steel, the steel industry improved not only the strength, but also the corrosion resistance and weldability of structural steel far beyond anything imagined by Rand in her Atlas Shrugged scenario.

According to Rand's thesis in *Atlas Shrugged*, these improvements were impossible. The new steels would have been banned by federal bureaucrats, just like Rand's fictional high-strength steel. But what actually happened? There was never the slightest governmental interference. Federal bureaucrats had nothing to do, pro or con, with the steel innovations. They were administered by a private organization, the American Institute of Steel Construction (AISC). The AISC simply incorporated the new steels into its revised *Manual of Steel Construction*, which has promulgated standards for structural steel's design, fabrication, and erection since 1921. Rand obviously didn't know that the AISC existed.

Rand's abysmal ignorance contrasts with the specialized knowledge systematically acquired by other novelists writing about industrial subjects. Arthur Hailey and John P. Marquand wrote novels requiring knowledge about various industries, and they sedulously learned how these industries operated. Explaining his research into the banking industry before writing his 1949 novel, *Point of No Return*, Marquand thanked a banker friend for getting him up to speed. Marquand's novel displays an impressive knowledge of a loan-officer's work.

Rand, however, had no interest in authentic presentation of the construction industry. The fabrication of her simple-minded propaganda required ignorance. If she had known anything about the construction industry, *Atlas Shrugged*'s preposterous myth would have been a deliberately concocted lie, not merely a product of ignorance. Any cult member or reader who accepts the validity of Rand's construction-industry myth necessarily shares her ignorance. Even a slight acquaintance with this knowledge would insulate a reader from Rand's ignorance.

I go into perhaps excessive detail here to hammer home the message: that Ayn Rand knew absolutely nothing about her chosen subject. She tells her readers nothing about the alloys used to strengthen her miracle steel. But her ignorance is greatest in her depiction of the evil bureaucracy deliberately thwarting technological progress. As a former structural engineer, who reported on the new alloy steels in 1962, I am as familiar with the construction industry as Rand was ignorant of it.

Rand's ignorance was tinged with hysteria. Here from a speech entitled "America's Persecuted Minority: Big Business," is her description of businessmen's travails in Kennedy administration's first year:

"If a small group of men were [sic] always regarded as guilty . . . regardless of the issues or circumstances involved, would you call it persecution? If this group were [sic] always made to pay for the sins, errors, or failures of any other group, would you call that persecution? If this group had to live under a special reign of terror, under special laws, from which all other groups were immune, laws which the accused could not grasp or define in advance and which the accuser could define in any way he pleased -- would you call that persecution" If this group were [sic] penalized, not for its faults, but for its virtues, not for its incompetence, but for its ability, not for its failure, but for its achievements -- would you call that persecution?

If the answer is 'yes' -- then ask yourself what sort of monstrous injustice you are condoning . ... That group is the American businessman."

Guilty as charged

Through her widespread influence since the publication of *Atlas Shrugged*, Rand helped to create the 2008 financial meltdown, which resulted in our extended recession. For two decades, Rand's disciple, former Federal Reserve Chairman Alan Greenspan, played a major role as the high priest of deregulation. As a prominent youthful member of the Rand cult, Greenspan was allegedly convinced by Rand that banks, like corporations in general, needed little or no government regulation. As even he now reluctantly admits, Greenspan's deregulating philosophy contributed mightily to the 2008 financial meltdown, via his support for President Bush's reckless tax cuts and deregulatory policies. Before the financial meltdown, Greenspan's youthful membership in the Rand cult was shrugged off as an amusing idiosyncrasy. But after the financial catastrophe struck, it was correctly assessed as an unheeded, but deadly warning. Widely viewed as an economic genius during the Bush 41, Clinton, and Bush 43 administrations, Greenspan was ultimately exposed as an intellectual fraud, a gullible victim of Rand's economic nonsense.

Prominent Republican politicians still profess to be Rand followers. Paul Ryan, chairman of the House Budget Committee, assigns *Atlas Shrugged* as required reading for his staffers. Ryan's presumed dedication to Rand reveals his hypocrisy. If he was a real disciple of Rand, Ryan would denounce federal aid for natural disasters -- tornados, hurricanes, floods, forest fires, and earthquakes. Yet he silently acquiesces to these anti-Randian government programs. Nothing in Rand's voluminous writings justifies federal disaster aid. She preached a consistent doctrine that would allow the poor to starve and the disaster-stricken to suffer misfortune unaided by government. In fact, Rand actively condemned aiding the poor as "immoral."

Rand owes her undeserved reputation as an innovative preacher of selfish rugged-individualism to Americans' historical ignorance. At its core, Rand's ideology is nothing more than Social Darwinism, the survival-of-the-fittest philosophy that thrived in the late 19ᵗʰ century. Championed by British philosopher Herbert Spencer, Social Darwinism was defended as the only dependable way to assure a thriving capitalist economy. Spencer denounced regulation and social programs benefitting the poor and middle-class as unwarranted — even immoral — interference with the natural order. According to Spencer, human society was analogous to the biological world. As Darwin's Theory of Evolution had allegedly demonstrated, biological evolutionary progress depends upon predators who perform the beneficial task of limiting, or even annihilating, the animal kingdom's unfit.

As the famed historian Richard Hofstadter explained in his brilliant book, *Social Darwinism in American Thought*, Spencer's doctrine drastically declined after Theodore Roosevelt instituted his progressive reforms prior to World War I. The American public had learned lessons taught by John D. Rockefeller and his fellow robber barons. Many Americans, especially in the Bible Belt, still need to learn this century-old lesson.

ABOUT THE AUTHOR

C.W. Griffin is a retired consulting engineer, currently free-lance writer, author of 10 predominantly technical books, but also general books –– notably TAMING THE LAST FRONTIER (on the 1970s' urban crisis) and CLEANING OUT CONGRESS: THE CASE FOR REFORM. His articles have appeared in Harper's, Atlantic Monthly, Washington Post, The Nation, The Progressive, The Reporter, and Saturday Review.